John Noake

A History of the Roman Catholics and Dissenters of Worcester

John Noake

A History of the Roman Catholics and Dissenters of Worcester

ISBN/EAN: 9783744664554

Printed in Europe, USA, Canada, Australia, Japan

Cover: Foto ©Lupo / pixelio.de

More available books at **www.hansebooks.com**

A HISTORY

OF THE

ROMAN CATHOLICS

OF

WORCESTER.

By *JOHN NOAKE*,

Author of *The Rambler*, &c.

LONDON: LONGMAN AND CO.
WORCESTER: J. NOAKE, HERALD OFFICE;
AND ALL BOOKSELLERS.
1861.
PRICE FIVE SHILLINGS.

DEDICATED, BY PERMISSION,

TO

JOSEPH WOOD, ESQ.,

Mayor of Worcester,

AND UNDER THE PATRONAGE OF HIS WORSHIP,

AS ALSO OF

THE RIGHT HON. EARL BEAUCHAMP,

R. PADMORE, ESQ., M.P.,

A. C. SHERRIFF, T. R. HILL, AND E. B. EVANS, ESQS.

"Men that are angry for *God*, passionate for *Christ*, that can call names for Religion and fling stones for Faith, may tell us they are Christians if they will, but nobody would know them to be such by their fruits. To be sure, they are no Christians of *Christ's* making."---*William Penn.*

Preface.

THE object for which this work was written is twofold: firſt, to preſerve and put in permanent form the records and materials for the hiſtory of each religious denomination in *Worceſter;* and, ſecondly, to inculcate humility and Chriſtian forbearance, by producing undeniable evidence that religious perſecution was not confined to any one body of Chriſtians, but was freely exerciſed by whatever party attained to power.

In carrying out this main deſign---which has occupied twelve months of cloſe reſearch and conſtant employment of the little leiſure afforded by an arduous profeſſion---many incidental reſults of an intereſting and uſeful kind have likewiſe been attained. More light has been thrown on the manners and cuſtoms of our anceſtors---

their thoughts, their religious opinions, their domestic and social life. Details have been preserved as to localities and now almost forgotten names of streets, habitations, and places of worship; besides lists (as far as possible) of the original members of each denomination in the city, many of whose descendants are still living, and brief biographies of departed ministers of the Gospel whose memories are had in reverence and esteem for their Christian worth and usefulness. A new version of some of the circumstances attending the Gunpowder Plot, translated from Jesuitical and other sources, with accounts of miracles and executions—which I have no doubt will be read with great interest—has been provided. The old house at *Hindlip*—one of the resorts of the conspirators—forms the subject of the frontispiece. That house was pulled down about forty years ago, to the great regret of all who valued antiquity and historical association; and the present mansion—a square brick building, its principal front having four Ionic pillars supporting an entablature—was erected.

I have also thought it desirable to commence each chapter with a brief account of the origin of the sect to which it is devoted, and to introduce so much of its general history as would be necessary to elucidate and explain the local materials now brought together; also to enliven the work with sketches and anecdotes of founders of sects, popular preachers, and others intimately or incidentally connected with the city (several of whom are still living), with specimens of their pulpit productions.

The great bulk of my material was new, and gathered from multifarious sources, as indeed the following pages will bear witness; the labour, therefore, has been very great for so small a result; yet I trust it will not be deemed unacceptable to the public.

Some of the records of which I have availed myself, there is reason to believe, would have been lost altogether but for my timely inquiries after them; now, however, by the aid and interposition of the printing press, such an accident would be rendered less regrettable, and this work I hope will be considered a trustworthy and permanent record and book of reference for each denomination whose history is brought under review.

Although I have not scrupled freely to express my opinions wherever I deemed it needful, this, I trust, will not be considered to detract from the merit of the work, as not a single word has been penned in bitterness of spirit or with a view to create animosity. The judicious *Hooker* was worthy of all praise when he predicted that " there would come a time when three words uttered with charity and meekness should receive a far more blessed reward than three thousand volumes written with disdainful sharpness of wit."

It will be observed that frequent mention is made of other towns and places in the county and district; but this is purely incidental, and to undertake the religious history of each town in the county would have been too colossal an undertaking for one whose time is so limited.

A copious index has been prepared, under the conviction that many books lose much of their value, as works of reference, from a lack of this very necessary adjunct.

On a digest of the facts brought together in this little production, I think my readers will agree with me in the expression of thankfulness that our lot has not been caſt in thoſe days when magiſtrates acted without law, juſtice, or humanity; when no religious and but little civil liberty exiſted; when ſuperſtition, ignorance, and a lack of many of the phyſical comforts we now enjoy, were the chief characteriſtics of ſociety in theſe iſlands.

Long prefaces being an abhorrence to me, it only now remains to expreſs my gratitude to the kind patrons whoſe names appear on the dedicatory page, and alſo to tender my acknowledgments to the following gentlemen, who kindly aſſiſted my literary labours, and afforded me facilities for the examination of records, &c. : Revs. *W. Waterworth*, *T. Dodd*, and *J. M'Owan;* Aldermen *T. R. Hill* and *Lewis;* Meſſrs. *Grove*, *Stanley Pumphrey*, *T. Baxter*, *Ward*, and *Vellacott*; as alſo to the librarians and authorities of the Britiſh Muſeum Library, and that of the Society of Antiquaries, Somerſet Houſe, in both of which noble inſtitutions I met with the utmoſt courteſy and kindneſs.

J. N.

Britannia Square, *Worceſter*,
December, 1860.

Index.

Abberley, ~~269.~~
~~Adams, 118.~~
~~Agreement, Baxter's, 92.~~
~~Alcester, 148, 161, 163,~~ 167,
~~285, 320.~~
Allen, Cardinal, 79.
~~Allen, Rev. J., 120.~~
~~All Saints, 98, 106.~~
~~Allies, 355, 359.~~
~~Alvechurch, 215.~~
Anderson, Father, 45, 47.
~~Andrew's, St., 99, 106, 110,
117, 118, 308, 325, 327,
359.~~
~~Areley Kings, 269.~~
~~Association Methodists, 340,
341.~~
Ashley, 26, 28, 37, ~~245.~~
Atkins, 55, 60, ~~110, 200.~~

Badley, Thomas, burning of, 1, 2.
Barlow, Dean, 5.
Battenhall, 6, 17.
Bayley, 60.
Bartholomew, St., 63.
Baptists, 36, 49, 52, 85, 89, ~~98, 100, 125, 145, 194, 198, 201, 216, 220, 236, 347.~~

Baxter, 69, ~~92, 93, 102, 106, et seq., 150, 154, 211, 212, 215.~~
Bartlett, Felix, 69, 70.
Bateman, 78.
~~Baker, 92, 99, 110.~~
~~Badland, Mr. T., 101, 102, 110, 111, 113, 115, 116.~~
~~Barker, Rev. T. R., 138.~~
~~Bartlett, Rev. J., 144.~~
~~Barebone, 150.~~
~~Battle of Worcester, 89, 209.~~
~~Bath, 249.~~
~~Bayfield, 364.~~
~~Backhouse, 286.~~
Baynham, Rev. J., 74.
Berry, Major-Gen., 50, ~~209.~~
Beswick, Father, 52.
Bedloe, 57.
Beeston, Father, 67, 69, 78.
Benedictines, 68.
Berkeley, 70, 71, 74.
~~Bewdley, 93, 109, 118, 154, 160, 161, 162, 171, 204, 317, 318, 324, 325, 328.~~
~~Berry, James, 106.~~
~~Bennett, 111, 144, 191, 198, 202, 204.~~
~~Belsham, 121, et seq.~~
~~Bentley, Horace, 136.~~

Bethania's Walks, 159, 165, 160.
Belsher, 162, 171, 172, 173, 179.
Bearcroft, Mr. P., 166.
Bedfordshire, 201.
Besse's Sufferings, 208, 220, 284, 236.
Beoley, 74.
Belbroughton, 230.
Bell, 303, 313.
Beesley, 278, 288.
Berridge, 354.
Bevington, 283, 288, 293.
Billinge, 72.
Bird, 78.
Birmingham, 121, 138, 171, 172, 310, 327.
Bishop Stortford, 140.
Biddulph, 347.
Bible Christians, 341.
Black Friars (Dominicans), 9.
Blount, Father, 41, 45.
Blackmoor Park, 68, 74.
Blockley, 93.
Blunt's *History of the Reformation*, 82.
Blackwell's *History of the Independents*, 105, 115, 121, 123.
Blackmore, 111, 116, 117, 118.
Bourne, 6, 14, 16, 17, 212, 223, 226, 231, 235, 236, 250, 252, 256, *et seq.*
Bonner, 17.
Boraston, John, 93.
Bosworth, Rev. F., 145.
Bourton, 148.

Boscobel, 63.
Bownas, 278.
Bolingbroke, 343.
Broad, R., 110.
Bromley, 27, 29, 33, 270.
Bromsgrove, 36, 60, 109, 159, 160, 161, 213, 258, 281, 294, 319.
Brownbill, 78.
Brown, 85, 86, 152, 357.
Brady, Thomas, 60.
Bristow, 78.
Bridgnorth, 106, 160.
Bristol, 129, 153, 154, 174, 181, 182, 191, 192, 193, 288, 308, 310, 324, 358.
Brettell Lane, 171.
Broadway, 228.
Drayton, 283.
Bradley, 363.
Burford, 40.
Butler, 60.
Burney, 73.
Burden, Mr. S., 115.
Butler, Mr. J., 116.
Burgess, 202, 293.
Burlingham, 288.
Byron, 338.

Catholics, 1, 89, 136.
Callowhill, Richard, 10.
Catesby, 26.
Calvin, 31, 86.
Campbell, Father, 53.
Case, William, 69.
Carroll, Archbishop, 71, 73.
Carr, 78.
Campion, 78.
Cathedral, 89, 92, 95.

Index. xiii

Calamy, 98, 100, 162, 164, 192.
Carpenter, Rev. J., 120.
Cartwright, 204.
Carlisle, 214.
Cambridge, 301.
Capper, 287.
Calvinistic Methodists, 341.
Challoner, Bishop, 22, 35, 39.
Chambers, 26, 159.
Chetle, 32, 113, 114.
Chaddesley, 61, 74.
Chepstow Grange, 63.
Chesterfield, 343.
Chichester, 346.
Cheltenham, 365.
Churchman, 281.
Cheshire, 284.
Church Lench, 93.
China manufactory, 102, 115.
Chadwick, 78.
City Library, 123, 124.
Chaines, 164, 193.
Clarke, 320, 335, 336.
Clifton-on-Teme, 217, 231.
Clement, 199.
Clough, Richard, 69, 70, 71.
Corbyn, 278, 287.
Cole, 325.
Collins, 326.
Cowell, 334.
Countess of Huntingdon's, 342.
Cox, 270.
Coppe, 147.
Cornwall, 152, 310.
Conventicle Act, 157.
Cooke, Rev. J., 137.
Collyer, Giles, 93.

Colles, Mr. Timothy, 118.
Commandery, 10.
Coughton, 22.
College, St. George's, 45.
Constable, Father, 61.
Collier, 63.
Corporation, 65, 104, 110, 322.
Cornthwaite, Rev. R., 74.
Cooper, 78.
Congregationalists, 81.
Coventry, 89, 95, 108, 147.
Crosby, 146, 153, 159.
Crowe, Rev. W., 176, 177, 178.
Crowder, 241, 254.
Crump, Jane, 313.
Crowle, 4, 5, 310.
Crosses, destruction of, 2.
Cromwell, 50, 87, 91, 92, 93, 108, 109, 110, 149, 199, 205, 206, 209.
Cross, Father, 71.

Davis, John, persecution of, 5.
Davies, 60, 177, 321, 355.
Dadmond, 63.
Day, 63, 305.
Danse, 106.
Daventry, 125.
Dawson, 171.
D'Assigny, 155.
Darke, Samuel, 177, 288, *et seq.*
Deans and Chapters, 15, 92.
Declaration of County against Sects, 89.
Declaration of Independents, 111.

Desborough, 63.
~~Dent and Co.'s glove manufactory, 118.~~
~~Derby, 148, 202, 205.~~
~~Dialogues of the Dead, 337.~~
~~Diggers, 150.~~
~~Doncaster, 207.~~
~~Doyle, Sir Francis, 92.~~
~~Doddridge, Dr., 86.~~
Dodd, 73, ~~143, 862.~~
Droitwich, 16, ~~204, 232, 233, 294, 310, 340.~~
~~Drury, Captain, 204.~~
Duckett, Jesuit, 42.
Dudley and Ward, Lord, 68.
Dudley, 77, ~~106, 108, 171, 232, 236, 281, 204, 294, 310, 324.~~
~~Durey, Mr. John, 93.~~

~~Eccles, 159, 161.~~
~~Edwards, 166.~~
~~Edmundson, 275, 328.~~
~~Ejectment of clergy in 1662, 98.~~
~~English, 348, 352.~~
~~Evans, 115, 325.~~
~~Evesham, 93, 118, 171, 192, 206 et seq., 214, 227, 281, 283, 294, 309, 310, 317, 318, 319, 324, 325, 356.~~
Executions, 2, 3, 24, 31, 37, 38, 39, 40, 41, 58, 60, ~~110.~~
Excommunications, 62.

~~Fawcett, 121.~~
Familists, 52.
~~Ferrers, 342.~~

~~Fenstanton, 155.~~
~~Feckman, Mr. T., 156, 162, 163, 232, 234.~~
~~Five-Mile Act, 157.~~
~~Fifth Monarchy Men, 220.~~
Fidoe, 254.
Fincher, 98, ~~109, 110, 114, 119, 230, 237, 238.~~
~~Firkins, 122.~~
Flanaghan, Canon, 22.
Floyd, John, 43.
~~Fleming, Rev. D., 129.~~
~~Fleetwood, Bishop, 257.~~
Forrest, Dr., burning of, 3.
~~Foley, 106, 109, 262, 270.~~
~~Foster, 135, 180, 186, et seq.~~
~~Follows, 283.~~
~~Fox, 147, 191, et seq., 213, 216, 217, 231, 238, et seq., 263.~~
Franciscans, or Grey Friars, 9, 67.
Friars of the Sack, 10.
Friars of the Holy Trinity, 10.
~~French, 352.~~
~~Fry, 287, 288.~~
~~Freebery, 317.~~

Garnett, 25, 26, 27, 28, 29, 31, 38, 40, 41.
Gabriel, John, 62.
~~Gas, introduction of, 173.~~
~~Garner, Samuel, 208.~~
~~Gamidge, 363.~~
Gerard, 25, 42.
George, St., Residence, 67.
Gibbon, 63, ~~344.~~
Gittings, Joseph, 75.

Index. xv

~~Gildas Salvianus, 100.~~
Gloucestershire, 60, ~~107,272,~~
~~297, 310, 311, 316, 317,~~
~~319, 320, 327.~~
~~Glasbrook, 316, 351, 352.~~
~~Glascott, 349, 352.~~
~~Glasgow, 129, 135, 136.~~
Goodman, 63.
Gordon, Lord George, 72.
~~Gosport, 176.~~
~~Gough, 273.~~
Grimley, 5.
Grimstead, West, 63.
Grafton Mission, 79.
~~Greenfield, Rev. T., 143.~~
~~Griffiths, 283.~~
Grafton Manor, 74.
~~Green, 352.~~
Gunpowder Plot, 26, 42.
Gunter, 63.
~~Gummer, Rev. J., 121.~~
~~Gurney, 287.~~

Hawford, Dean, 5.
Habingdon, 24, *et seq.*
Hagley, 26, 40, ~~309.~~
Hall, 27, 63, ~~135, 143, 160,~~
~~174, 180, et seq.~~
Hassells, 44.
Harley, Sir E., 66.
Harvington, 73, 74.
Hawkins, Mr. J., 73.
Hanley Castle, 68.
Harrison, John, 79.
~~Hancock, 88.~~
~~Hartlebury, 93, 269.~~
~~Hand, 111, 116.~~
~~Hathaway, Elisha, 166, 167,~~
~~169, 170, 172, 179.~~

~~Haines, 238, 262.~~
~~Halesowen, 309.~~
~~Hampton, 318.~~
~~Hardwick, 339.~~
~~Hayes, 352.~~
~~Havergal, 355.~~
~~Harris, 363.~~
~~Haigh, 365.~~
Heath, Bishop, 12.
Herefordshire, 24, 52, 53,
66, ~~124, 154, 161, 168,~~
~~178, 283.~~
~~Hewlings, 862.~~
~~Helen's, St., 202.~~
Hindlip, 24, 26, 27, 29, 33,
38, 63.
Highmeadow, 63.
~~Higgins, Abigail, 117.~~
~~Hill, Alderman T. R., 143.~~
~~Hide, Judge, 222.~~
~~Himbleton, 255.~~
~~Hill, Rowland, 301, 348, 349,~~
~~352, 357, et seq.~~
Holbech, Henry, last Prior, 5.
Holt, 14, 17.
Holbeach, 26.
Hornyold, Dr., 68, 74.
Holden, 78.
~~Hopkins, G., 93.~~
~~Holdsworth, Dean, 96.~~
~~Howell, 97.~~
~~Hooper, Bishop, 106.~~
~~Hedges, Mr. T., 120.~~
~~Hoxton, 134.~~
~~Hook, Dean, 136.~~
~~Hook Norton, 148, 161.~~
~~Holder's MS., 167, 168, 169.~~
~~Honeybourne, 317, 319.~~
~~Howarth, 284.~~

xvi   Index.

Hooker, 311.
Humberton, Henry, 63.
Hume, 86.
Hurndall, Rev. Dr., 140,
    143, 144.
Humphrys, Mr. R., 164.
Huntingdon, Countess of,
    207.
Hughes, 335.
Hurd, Bishop, 351, 356.
Huddington, 26.

Images, destruction of, 2, 7,
    20, 66.
Independents, 49, 81, 157,
    162, 172, 194, 214, 220,
    347.
Inghamites, 341.

Jarrett, 78.
Jacob, Henry, 85.
Jackson, Eleazar, 88
Jay, Rev. W., 135.
James, Rev. J. A., 135.
Jesuits, 21, 63.
Jenks, Roland, 23.
Jeffries, Judge, 98.
Jones, 29, 30, 345, 347, 352.
Jordan, Patrick, 60.
Johnson, 104, 119, 288.
John's, St., 340.
Juvency, 24, 26.
Juice, or Jewkes, 92, 100,
    -109.
Judgment of Associated Mi-
    nisters, 93.

Kemble, Father, 53.
Kensington, 129.

Kerr and Binns, 313.
Kempsey, 340.
King's evil, 63.
Kirk, Scottish, 85.
Kidderminster, 93, 106, 107,
    108, 110, 117, 121, 143,
    211, 212, 215, 294, 310,
    318, 326, 334, 356.
King's Norton, 212.
Kingswood, 301.
Kingston, 335.
King, 335.
Knott, Ed., 47.
Knox, John, 85.
Knapp, Susan, 314, 330, 339.
Knight, 226, 253.

Lady Huntingdon's, 342.
Lake, 339, 357, 362, 364.
Latimer, at Dr. Forrest's
    burning, 105.
Lavender, 60.
Laurenson, 78.
Lane, James, 79.
Laslett, 143.
Lavington, 309.
Launceston, 202.
Leigh, 20, 340.
Levison, Father, 57.
League and covenant, 48.
Lechmere, 116.
Ledbury, 118, 121, 154.
Lewis, 122, 335, 365.
Leifchild, 137, 174.
Levellers, 150.
Leominster, 154, 159, 161,
    166, 171.
Log-of-mutton Baptists, 155.
Leicester, 168, 192, 200.

Index. xvii

Lichfield, 106.
Liturgy of Church, 346.
Lister, Thomas, 25.
Llandaff, Bishop of, 20.
Lloyd, Bishop, 267.
Lovelace, Lord, 48.
Lomax, 78.
Lower, 338, et seq.
Longevity among the Quakers, 290.
Lowe, 208.
Lyttelton, 26, 27, 29, 30, 40, 47, 337, 343.
Lynes, 286.

Maunders, 63.
Macaulay, 68.
Malvern, 69, 74, 294, 309, 324.
Mace, John, 79.
Martin's, St., 102, 115.
Martin, 115, 143, 144, 208.
Mail-coach, first in Worcester, 248.
Martley, 266.
Marlborough, 343.
Madan, 347.
Manchester, 300.
Marriages, Quaker, 251.
M'Clune, 78.
Merror, 352.
Meagher, 78.
Methodism, 297.
Militia Service and the Quakers, 289.
Midland Association (Baptist), 157, 161, 163, 168, 170.

Mirabilis Annus, 96.
Michael's, St., 11, 12.
Miracles, 32, 34, 35, 36, 38, 39, 40, 41, 59, 97, 200.
Mitton, Edward, 32.
More, Prior, 4.
Moore's Anglican Mission, 36, 43, 45.
Monmouth, 63, 324.
Moseley, 72.
Morris, John, 75.
Morgan, Rev., 76.
Morton, W., 79.
Moore, Mr. Simon, 92, 97, 98, 107, 109, 110.
Mosheim, 145, 180.
Moreton, 148, 161.
Mormonism, 178.
More, Hannah, 301.
M'Owan, 339.

Nanfan, Mr. J., 110.
Nailor, James, 192, 193.
Nash, 63, 88, 102, 343.
Neal, 280.
New Connexion Methodists, 341.
Newell, 352.
Newman, 77, 115, 260.
Nind, 317.
Nicholas, St., 61, 98, 100, 110, 126, 128, 257, 260, 262, 270.
Norwich, 79, 355.
Norton, 9, 340.
North, Robert, 42.

Oates, 52, 62, 147.
Oldcorn, 25, *et seq.*

xviii *Index.*

Oldbury, 111, 283.
Oliver, 25, 38, 40, 63, 69, 70, 75.
Omer's, St., 43, 47, 67.
Ombersley, 164, 236, 310.
Orton, Job, 86, 124.
Oswald's, St., 10, 53, 58, 59, 70, 75, 79.
Oscot College, 76.
Osborn, Rev. G., 124, 125, 128, 129.
Oswen, John, 146.
Owen, 23, 35, 37, 41, 803.
Owen, Dr. John, 86.
Oxford, 23, 52, 66, 69, 78, 96, 147, 154, 297, 300, 301.

Pate, Bishop, 20.
Pakington, 54, 61, 236, 237, 270.
Parker, 74, 258, et seq.
Padmore, Alderman, 140, 365.
Palmer's Nonconformists' Memorial, 152.
Pardoe, 158, 164, 165, 168, 233, 234, 235, 252, 259, 261, et seq., 273, 275, 276, 277.
Page, Henry, 173.
Payton, 236, 237, 254, 280, 281, 284.
Peter's, St., 14, 294.
Persons, Father, 21, 43.
Percy, 26.
Perks, 40.
Peters, Hugh, 88, 89.
Penn, Wm., 191, 192, 193.

Pershore, 107, 169, 171, 174, 189, 231, 283, 294, 318, 320.
Pittaway, 207.
Plymouth, 153, 161.
Plymouth Brethren, 177.
Popham, Attorney-General, 43.
Potter, Dean, 47, 96.
Powick, 88, 107.
Postlewhite, 78.
Poynting, 170.
Powell, 140.
Prattenton, Dr., 49.
Price, 49, 327, 365.
Protestant Association, 50.
Presbyterians, 84, 91, 92, 96, 101, 111, 116, 122, 128, 157, 214, 240, 336.
Priddey, Roland and John, 104, 119.
Prisons in Worcester, 219.
Primitive Methodists, 340.
Protestant Methodists, 341.
Priory of Worcester surrendered, 4.
Prestwood, 26.
Purshall Hall, 74.
Pusey, 77.
Pump Street Independents, 122.
Pumphrey, 288.
Pye, Parson, 63.

Quakers, 36, 52, 98, 101, 150, 156, 158, 191, 327, 336, 347.

Rainsborough, Colonel, 108.

Ranters, 150, 340.
Randolph, 58.
Red Hill, 39, 58, 59.
Relics of Priory furniture, 8.
Residence, Catholic, 45.
Records, 60, 111, 162, 208, 231, 238, 249, 316, 321.
Registers, 62, 70, 115, 171.
Redmarley, 68.
Restoration of Charles II, 51, 96, 156, 217.
Reading, 100.
Reynolds, 111.
Redford, Rev. Dr., 115, 134, et seq., 177.
Redditch, 294, 310.
Reforming Methodists, 340, 341.
Rhyd, The, 116.
Riding House, 312.
Rigby, 78.
Robinson, Rev. A., 74, 76.
Rouselench, 20.
Rogers, 55.
Romish hierarchy restored, 78.
Robinson, 85.
Ross, 154.
Rudda, 316.
Routh, 204.
Romaine, 345.
Roberts, 363.
Russell, Father, 67.
Rugeley, 287.

Salisbury, 154, 246.
Sandys, 17, 20, 164, 236, 287.
Sarjeant, Rev. R., 10.

Sanders, Father, 52.
Saracen's Head inn, 60.
Sanders, 71, 170.
Sandwich, 164.
Sanderson, 364.
Sedgley Park, 68.
Sewell, N., 76.
Seekers, 151.
Sewell's History of Quakers, 222, 286.
Sellen, 352.
Sheldon, 17.
Shelley, Mrs., 44.
Shelsley, 269.
Shewring, Mayor, 64.
Shropshire, 69, 108, 171, 232, 284, 294, 318, 325.
Shipston, 254, 294.
Shillitoe, 286.
Shirley, 349, 350.
Shelsley, preaching hour glass, 49.
Shrines, 7.
Silisdon, Father, 47.
Siege of Worcester, 89.
Skinner, 322, 348.
Slater, Mr. S., 93.
Smith, Sidney, 75.
Smith, Dr. Pye, 135.
Smith, Humphrey, 207.
Smith, Robert, 220, 222, 223, 224, 236, 237, 254.
Smithen's Green, 340.
Socinians, 121.
Somerset, 190, 204.
Soley, Mayor, 256.
Sortes Virgilianæ, 307.
Spilsbury, 109, 117, 118, 121.

Spetchley, 74.
~~Squib in 1646, 90.~~
Stoneyhurst, 40.
~~Stowell's History of Puritans, 97.~~
~~Stokes, 116, et seq.~~
~~Sturmer, 178.~~
~~Street, 244, 245.~~
~~Stage coach, first in Worcester, 248.~~
~~Stourbridge, 254, 284, 294.~~
~~Stourport, 318, 329, 334, 335.~~
~~Story, 275.~~
~~Stanton, 280.~~
~~Stephenson, 208.~~
Stillingfleet, 66, ~~152, 300, 343.~~
~~Stevens, 338.~~
~~Steel, 365.~~
Stanford, 48.
Staffordshire, 79, ~~127,~~ 171.
Sugar, John, 24.
~~Sunday school, first in Worcester, 126.~~
Swithin's, St., 10, ~~359.~~
Swale, 78.
~~Swift, 159, 270.~~
~~Symonds, Mr. G., 156,~~ 220.
~~Sympson, William,~~ 192, 214, ~~241, 245.~~

~~Taylor, 353.~~
Talbot, Hon. James, 67.
~~Terril, Judge, 222.~~
~~Tewkesbury, 148, 161, 176, 171, 208, 217, 275, 281, 283, 286, 312, 317, 323, 324.~~

~~Teakes, 149.~~
Test and Corporation Acts, 68, ~~157.~~
~~Thurlow, 280.~~
~~Thorpe, Rev., 129.~~
~~Thornburgh, Mr. Giles, 95.~~
Thomas, Bishop, 64.
Thornborough, Bishop, 45.
~~Tibberton, 848.~~
Townsend, 47, 52, ~~89, 90, 96, 156, 220.~~
~~Tomkins, 110.~~
~~Tom's Coffee House, 121.~~
~~Tombes, 147, 152, 153, 154, 159, 190, 233, 236.~~
~~Toleration Act, 161, 345.~~
Trinity Guild, 9.
Tristram, Rev. J., 76.
~~Trebell, Jos., 92.~~
~~Tredington, 238, 244, 254, 285.~~
~~Turner, 243.~~
~~Trevecca College, 348, 351.~~
~~Trowbridge, 364.~~
~~Twittey, 245, 248.~~
~~Tyringham, Prebendary, 96.~~

~~Underhill, 16, 17, 155.~~
~~Uniformity, Act of, 97, 100, 228.~~
~~Upton, 161, 171, 311, 320.~~
Urwick, Rev. T., 120, 121.
~~Uxbridge, 135.~~

Vaughan, 73, ~~129, 130, 136.~~
~~Venner's Insurrection, 220.~~
~~Vernon, 266.~~
~~Venn, 349.~~

Index.

Wall, Father, *alias* Webb, 53.
Walpole, 67.
Walmesley, William, 70.
Walsh, 76, ~~209, 270.~~
Ward, 77, ~~262.~~
~~Wandsworth, 85.~~
~~Watts, Dr. Isaac, 86.~~
~~Warmstry, Dean, 95.~~
~~Warren, 111.~~
Warwickshire, 24, ~~120, 147, 148, 161, 294, 310.~~
~~Waters, Thomas, 174, 175.~~
~~Waite, Rev. J. J., 178.~~
~~Wardley, 364.~~
Waterworth, Father, 67, 78.
~~Walker, 298.~~
Wesley, 71, ~~297, et seq., 343, 352.~~
Weedall, 76.
Weetman, Clement, 79.
~~Wesleyans, 122, 207.~~
~~West Bromwich, 124; 125.~~
~~Westminster, 143.~~
~~Westmancote, 152.~~
~~Westcombe, 202.~~
Wharton, 71, 72.
White Ladies, 9, 10.
~~White Lady Aston, 152.~~
~~Whalley, Colonel, 108.~~
~~Whitefield, 125, 297, 300, et seq., 343, et seq., 352.~~
~~Whitehead, George, 216.~~
Whetstone, Roger, 36.
Wilson, Dean, 15.
Winter, 16, 17, 26, 30, 40.
Winifred, St., 35.

Williams, 74, 75, ~~157, 176.~~
~~Wilson's Pilgrim Fathers, 83.~~
~~Willenhall, 101, 110.~~
~~Withers, Sir C. T., 117.~~
~~Windsor, 134, 239.~~
~~Wigley, 144, 290.~~
~~Willoughby, carpenter, 172.~~
~~Wincheomb, 187.~~
~~Wichenford, 254.~~
~~Winnington, 270.~~
~~Wilberforce, 301.~~
~~Wilks, 352.~~
Winkworth, 352.
~~Wills, 353.~~
Witley Court, ~~365.~~
Wolverhampton, 52, 68, ~~310.~~
~~Wootton-under-Edge, 122.~~
~~Working Man's Institute, 124.~~
Wombourn, 72.
~~Wormington, 327.~~
~~Woods, 364.~~
~~Wood, Mayor, 365.~~
~~Wright, Thomas, 93.~~
Wylde's Lane, 10.
Writtle Park, 63.
~~Wyld, 121, 218, 227, 230, 231, 232, 246.~~
~~Wyatt's Hospital, 256.~~

Yate, Dame Mary, 62.
~~Yardley, 104,~~ 21.
~~Young, Mayor of Evesham, 211.~~
Yorkshire, 25, ~~200, 201, 204, 328.~~
Young, Francis, 78.

WORCESTER

—o—

The Catholics.

"THE true spirit is to search after GOD and for another life with lowliness of heart; to fling down no man's altar, to punish no man's prayer; to heap no penalties and no pains on those solemn supplications which, in divers tongues, and in varied forms, and in temples of a thousand shapes, but with one deep sense of human dependence, men pour forth to GOD."---SYDNEY SMITH.

N few *English* cities were more important changes effected by the great religious Reformation than in *Worcester*. The principles of *Wickliffe* had taken root here long before *Henry VIII* had acquired for himself the title of "Defender of the Faith," and the public mind had been gradually prepared for that religious movement which was cradled in *Germany* but attained its fullest development in this island. As early as the year 1409, *Thomas Badley*, a tailor of *Worcester*, was arraigned before the

Bishop and convicted of heresy because he denied that any priest could make the body of *Christ* sacramentally. He said "it was ridiculous to imagine that *Christ* at His last supper held His own body in His hand and brake and divided it; and if every consecrated host was *Christ's* body, then there must be in *England* no less than 20,000 gods." After this he was examined before the Archbishop of *Canterbury*, and great pains were taken to make him recant, but without effect, and the Archbishop confirmed the sentence of his Right Rev. brother of *Worcester*; whereupon *Badley* was burnt at Smithfield. The Prince of *Wales* was present on the occasion, and having compassion on the man, he caused the fire to be extinguished, and offered *Badley* a pension if he would recant, but the poor man continued firm in his faith, and so was burnt.

In 1522 the high cross before *Worcester* Guildhall was defaced, though the local records do not state whether this was a demonstrative act of the *Worcester* population, or done by order of the civic rulers. It was sixteen years later that the images of *Walsingham*, with those of *Ipswich*, *Worcester*, *Welsdon*, and other places, were taken to *London* and burnt at *Chelsea*; and some thirty or forty years afterwards that "the high cross over against the *Worcester* toll-shop" and others at the Cathedral and the

"Grafs-crofs" were ordered to be taken down. In 1535, *Henry* declared war againſt the pretenſions of the Pope, and ordered the Earl of *Eſſex* to inſtitute meaſures for apprehending all prieſts and curates who " ſet forth and extolled the juriſdiction and authority of the Biſhop of *Rome*, otherwiſe called Pope." No one can now reaſonably ſuppoſe that *Henry* had changed his religious principles---if he ever poſſeſſed any---only on one radical point he differed from the Catholic body, viz., in preferring himſelf to exerciſe the office of Pope, that his brutal and filthy paſſions might be indulged without check or reſtraint. Among the early victims of that reign, a friar named Dr. *Forreſt* was condemned for denying the royal ſupremacy; a large wooden ſtatue of the virgin was brought from *Wales* to make the death-fire, and *Latimer*, Biſhop of *Worceſter*, preſided at the execution. While preaching to the poor friar, as he hung ſuſpended in the flames, the Biſhop exceeded his uſual eloquence, and aſked the half-conſumed victim what ſtate he would die in; but the friar, in a bold voice, anſwered, "that if an angel ſhould come down from heaven and teach him any other doctrine than he had received and believed from his youth, he would not now believe him;" and ſo he was hanged and burnt. Perhaps this incident (given on the authority of *Stowe's*

Annales), of a Proteftant Bifhop of *Worcefter* prefiding at the execution of a friar, will be new to many of my readers; but one object of this work is to prove that religious perfecution was not confined to Catholics or any other fect of Chriftians; it was the weapon ufed by all who attained to a predominance in the ftate; it was the fpirit of the age and not of a party: Bifhop *Jewell* himfelf, one of the bright lights of the Reformation, approved the theory of burning heretics, as alfo to a certain extent did *Jeremy Taylor*, who was a great champion of religious liberty.

In the vifitation of the monafteries *Latimer* was extremely active, and in the year 1539 the Benedictines of *Worcefter* Priory put on fecular habits and furrendered, after their order had been in poffeffion of the church of *Worcefter* for 570 years. All our cathedral priories, except *Carlifle*, and moft of the richeft abbeys in *England*, were held by Benedictines. *William More*, the then Prior of *Worcefter*, had forefeen the coming ftorm, and fagacioufly made terms with the mammon of unrighteoufnefs, refigning his comfortable poft on condition that he fhould enjoy *Crowle* Houfe (about four miles from *Worcefter*) with plate, linen, and furniture, and occafional lodgings at the priory, the keep of two geldings, fuel at *Worcefter* and *Crowle*, a monk to wait on him, a pension of 50*l.* per annum, 1000 marks down on the nail, and the payment of all his debts, which amounted to 100*l.* *Green* says that he had also the manor of *Grimley*. The house to which the ex-prior retired is still in existence, near the church at *Crowle*, and his coffin-slab may be found, after some difficulty, in the interior of the church. *Henry Holbech*, alias *Randes*, was the last nominal prior; he had been consecrated Bishop-suffragan of *Worcester*, with the title of Bishop of *Bristol*, and on the surrender of the priory he was appointed the first Dean, and subsequently Bishop of *Rochester* and *Lincoln*. *John Barlow* succeeded him as Dean in 1544; and in 1553, *Philip Hawford*, the last Abbot of *Evesham*, became Dean in return for having surrendered so easily his own abbey some years before. All this was but a change of name, and a promotion of pliable men in the place of those who maintained on principle that *Henry* was not *de jure* the head of the church of *Christ* in these realms. The creed and ceremonials of the church had undergone but little variation, nor had the Romish spirit of persecution died out at this early period of our transitional progress; for I find that, in the last year of this king's reign, a lad of twelve years of age, named *John Davis* (nephew of *Thomas Johnson*, an apothecary of *Worcester*), for reading the *Testament* and other good English books, was horribly treated in a dungeon at the *Worcester* Guildhall, called "the Peephole," after having been removed from the cell into which he was first put, and where they tested his powers of endurance by holding his finger in a candle, but, as the historian gravely assures us, " without any visible effect upon the finger or the boy's form of mind." He was then put in iron bolts, and made to lie on the cold damp ground, with only two sheepskins to cover him, nor allowed to be visited by any of his friends. The Papists (says the chronicler, *Fox*, in his *Book of Martyrs*) made great threats at him, and even put a madman for his companion, who threatened his life with a large knife. The poor boy was to have been tried before the Judges, but ere their arrival the King went to his long account, " and the force of the law was stayed." *Davis* was nevertheless arraigned before the Judges, *Portman* and *Marven*, who ordered him to be whipped, but a Mr. *Bourne* (afterwards Sir *John Bourne*, Secretary of State, who resided at *Battenhall*), declared to the Judges that he had had whipping enough, and then took him to his house and well treated him, but at last put him away for fear he should infect their son *Anthony* with heresy. *Davis* afterwards became " a profitable minister in the Church of England." This account, written by *Davis* himself, is abridged in *Fox's Martyrs*, but has been recently published in full by the Camden Society, and ably edited by my excellent friend, Mr. *John Gough Nichols*, F.S.A.

The shrines of St. *Oswald* and St. *Wulstan*, in *Worcester* Cathedral, had been taken down in 1538, and the bones of the saints, together with those of Bishop de *Constantiis*, were wrapped in lead and buried at the north side of the high altar---a sufficient indication that the relics of those great men were expected to interfere no more in human affairs, and might now rest in peace with the ashes of their fathers. For the first time on Candlemas Day, 1547, no candles were hallowed or borne, nor were ashes hallowed on Ash Wednesday; the high altar was taken down to the ground in 1551; and on May 13th, 1560, Bishop *Sandys* began his visitation at *Worcester*, when the crucifix and images of Our Lady were burnt in the yard of the Cathedral. The image of Our Lady was a very large one, and had been held in great reverence, but when stripped of the veils that covered it, our reformers found out that it was a statue of a bishop, ten feet high! By that time, not only had the Papal dominion come to an end in England, but the religion of which His Holiness was the chief hierarch had ceased to be the professed religion of the English nation; the odours of its incense had evaporated, and the glories of its splendid altars faded away; its processions and pageants no longer delighted the masses of the people, and the functions of its vast and complicated machinery ceased their movements. Then were crosses, chalices, censers, and pyxes, made into silver pots and cups "for the communion table," or useful vessels "for Mr. Dean and common hospitality;" while copes and vestments were transformed into coverings for the communion table or cushions for the choir and church. In an inventory of the Priory furniture at the Dissolution, among other things are the following:

"Item, Seynt *Oswalde* and Seynt *Ulstans* hede with selvr and gylte---a myter for Seynt *Oswalde* hede---with stonys set ther ynn, a arme of Seynt *Edmunde* the Bysshoope, ii woode coveryde with selver gylte,---a arme of Seynt *Romane* the Bysshope coveryde yn certen placis with selver, ii small fryms---gylte with lyttle stonys yn the wiche ther bynn certen relyquis of Seynt *Oswalde* and Seynt *Wlsta*—coveryde with selvr, a moyle of Seynt Oswalde una vitta cirra caput Ste *Margarete*---with selver, with other garnyssynge with selver abowte the hede, xi thousande V'gyns, in parte of a skul---of *Herfford's* tombe garnyssyde in golde and gylte with ii rynges, ii old pannes of xvi galands, a pe—— basen to tempr wax ther yn, a tryvett."

Thus was the genius of Popery unrobed, and

"with sighing sent" from all her ancient groves.
The friars, too, shared no better fate than their
brethren the monks, for among other establish-
ments broken up in *Worcester* at the Reformation
were---

1.---The Franciscans or Grey Friars, founded
by a *Beauchamp*, some relics of which establishment, especially the refectory, remained till within
living memory on the site of the present City
Gaol. At the Suppression, this establishment was
granted to the bailiffs and citizens of *Worcester*,
who paid yearly a rent to the crown.

2.---The Dominicans, or Black (preaching)
Friars, whose house was situate at the back of
Broad Street, also founded by a *Beauchamp* of
Powick, about the time of *Edward III*. In the
twenty-first year of that reign they had a grant
of a piece of ground within the city walls, called
" Bellasses," to build their house upon. At the
Dissolution, this house was also granted to the
bailiffs and citizens of *Worcester*.

3.---The Trinity Guild; founded by *Richard
Norton*, 45th of *Edward III*, being a brotherhood
or charity of three priests or chaplains, to sing
mass perpetually for the soul of the founder and
for all Christian souls, and to help the parson and
curate of the parish church in time of need,
"because it doth abound of houseling people."
At the Dissolution it passed into various hands,
and the Trinity Hall became the property of the
corporation of weavers, walkers, and clothiers.

4.---The White Ladies' Nunnery, founded by
a Bishop of *Worcester* before the Norman con-

quest. If I mistake not, the present worthy incumbent of St. *Swithin's* still receives a portion of his income as chaplain or father confessor to these poor white ladies, who have so long formed one of the unrealities of life; former incumbents were their confessors, and at the suppression of the nunnery it was granted to *Richard Callowhill*, and the site is now held under the governors of Queen *Elizabeth's* School in this city, while a portion of its income was secured to St. *Swithin's* living. Of course, should the Protestant establishment take a monastic turn, the Rev. *R. Sarjeant* and his successors will have to do duty in the confessor line, for value already received.

5.—St. *Oswald's*, established for monks infected with leprosy, afterwards changed into a lodging house for the wayfarer, and subsequently into almshouses, was *not* dissolved at the Reformation, but merely transferred into the Protestant custody of the Dean and Chapter.

6.—The Commandery, founded by St. *Wulstan* in Norman times, as a religious order of St. *Augustine*, professing chastity, poverty, and obedience. The masters of this order assumed the title of *præceptores*, or commanders, and hence the name of the establishment, which has remained to this day. Soon after the Dissolution, the house and its possessions were conveyed to *T. Wylde*, clothier, from whence Wylde's Lane takes its name.

7.—Chantries in many of the parish churches.

8.—A "Convent of *Fratres de pænitentia Jesu Christi*," or "Friars of the Sack," made a settlement here *temp. Henry III;* and some "Friars of the Holy Trinity, for the redemption of captives," were said to have been located between Angel Lane and Broad Street, but I have met with no information whether these were in existence at the time of the Reformation.

In the first year of *Edward VI* the council issued injunctions for removing images from all churches, and during a general visitation the rosary and mass were doomed; the Bishops and clergy were summoned to take the oath of allegiance and to make use of the new book of homilies and *Erasmus's Paraphrase*. In the month of November after *Henry's* death, at the meeting of Parliament, mass was sung in English for the first time. The *Worcester* parochial records do not go back to this date except the books of St. *Michael's* parish, in which the progress of the Reformation under the young King is distinctly set forth. A man was employed in that little church to hew down the images and whitelime the walls; the holy water pot and certain organ pipes were sold for 2s. 10d., and all other furniture appertaining to the exploded ceremonies was disposed of at what would be called (in modern drapers' slang) "an alarming sacrifice." Moreover, the churchwardens and their friends, who made out an inventory on the occasion, took care to make merry at a tavern over the fallen fortunes of the old dispensation and the brighter advent of the new. Boards on trestles were substituted for the altar, and instead of sculptured saints and fenestral emblazonment, a man was engaged to write the Scriptures (on the walls) and paint the church at 2*d.* per yard.

Desperate efforts were at that time made in *Devonshire* and other counties to restore the old religion, and the Catholics opposed the King's preachers to the face; but their attempts were uniformly defeated. *Heath*, then Bishop of *Worcester*, had protested against the new ordinal and form of ordination drawn up by virtue of an Act of Parliament, and refusing to subscribe thereto he was sent to the Fleet and deprived of his bishopric, *Hooper* being his successor.

At Queen *Mary's* accession to the throne, the altars of the proscribed faith were again erected; and the crysmatory, censer, and pyx, once more appeared in the inventory of St. *Michael's* church, with the pascal taper, wax, and frankincense. To the credit of many of the bishops in *Mary's* reign be it recorded that they had but little stomach for superintending the sanguinary scenes which then disgraced the English rule, and generally they left all the work and wickedness to others, as at Bristol, to *Dalby*, the chancellor, who appears to have been so fond of the fiery element in this world that it is hoped his earthly tastes have not been consulted in that to which he has since gone.* Indeed it has been justly

* See the *Bristol Church-goer.*

said, that we can hardly credit history or our senses, at this distance of time, to think that there could have been a period in our annals, or a people amongst our ancestors, when and by whom such wanton and insane cruelties could have been perpetrated. But these acts of *Mary's* time were only the temporary glare thrown out by a dying flame. The five years' resuscitation of the old faith had probably done more than all previous experiences to confirm the national abhorrence of Popery, nor did the blood of Protestants so freely shed during that brief period appeal to heaven in vain. The knell of the *Romish* creed in *England* was rung and the day of retribution was at hand. Nevertheless all good Christians must regard with horror the vindictive violence with which the nation avenged itself on a persecuting priesthood, fallen from power. Christian charity might have suggested to our Puritan forefathers the exercise of that toleration and forbearance which they had sought in vain at the hands of men whose creed necessarily enforced the extermination of heretics. But, alas for human weakness, the truth must be told, even if it disabuse many a Protestant reader of fondly cherished hallucinations, begotten by one-sided histories, written from a stand-point of the grossest partiality. *Mosheim* says it is an observation often made, that all religious sects, when they are kept under and oppreffed, are remarkable for inculcating the duties of moderation, forbearance, and charity, towards thofe who diffent from them, but that as foon as the fcenes of perfecution are removed, and they in their turn arrive at power and preëminence, they forget their own precepts and maxims, and leave both the recommendation and practice of charity to thofe who groan under their yoke.

With the acceffion of Queen *Elizabeth* (1558) commences the real hiftory of the perfecution of the Catholics in this country; and thofe who inveftigate that hiftory with fairnefs cannot but admit that, whether in reference to the Catholic clergy or laity, more noble examples of heroic fortitude, patience, long-fuffering, and unyielding avowal of what they believed to be the truth, have never been prefented in any period of the world's hiftory or in any phafe of "man's inhumanity to man." It is probable that at this period the two great religious parties---the Catholics and all who diffented from them---were nearly equal in numbers throughout the country, and it may be readily imagined that antagoniftic feelings everywhere pervaded fociety to an extent almoft fubverfive of focial order and individual fecurity. Inftances of this occurred at *Worcefter*. Sir *John Bourne*, of *Holt* Caftle, lord of the manor of *Battenhall* (St. *Peter's* parifh, *Worcefter*), who was one of the principal Secretaries of State in the time of *Mary*, and a great enemy to the Reformation and the Proteſtant Biſhops, is ſaid in *Strype's Annals* to have inſulted Mrs. *Wilſon*, wife of the Dean of *Worceſter*, in 1563, and the wife of a prebendary, by taunting them with being the wives of prieſts---a condition which the Catholic party looked upon as little better than one of adultery ; and a violent affray took place between the ſervants of the reſpective parties in conſequence. In *Strype's* relation great ſtreſs is laid upon the fact that Mrs. *Wilſon* was a gentlewoman, and hence the inference that Sir *John Bourne* was "no gentleman." Dr. *Wilſon*, the huſband of this lady, was one of the judges at Frankfort, in 1557, to decide the religious diſputes which began to ariſe among the refugees, and giving origin to that diſſenſion which afterwards ſo miſerably rent and divided the Church of *England*. Here he was diſtinguiſhed among the principal divines who exerted their abilities on the occaſion, his name being ſubſcribed to a plan for amending their diſcipline. In 1562-3 he was choſen by the Dean and Chapter of *Worceſter* to repreſent them in the *Weſtminſter* Aſſembly; and although he would have gone further in the abolition of what he conſidered Popiſh remains, when it was carried againſt him he did not deem theſe indifferent things a ſufficient ground to justify his separation from the Established Church. He voted for the famous six articles: 1. To abolish all holy days except those of *Christ* and Sundays; 2. For the minister in time of prayer to turn his face to the people; 3. To omit the cross in baptism; 4. To leave to the discretion of the Ordinary the order of kneeling at the communion; 5. For the minister to use the surplice only in time of divine service and the sacraments, and that no minister officiate but in a comely garment (this was meant to alter the sacerdotal habits further from those used in the *Romish* Church); and, 6. To remove organs out of churches. These articles were thrown out of the lower house by a majority of only one.

Sir *John Bourne* was also known as the persecutor (in the time of Queen *Mary*) of Mr. *Edward Underhill*, a Protestant, one of the band of Gentlemen Pensioners, and nephew of *Robert Winter*, of *Wych*, county of *Worcester*. When the said *Underhill* was examined before the council on a charge of making "a ballatt against ye Papistes," he seems to have had the best of the argument with Sir *John*. The latter admitted that *Underhill* had come of a "worshipful house in *Worcestershire*," and regretted that he was "a heritike knave," and had "spent his levynge wantonly." *Underhill* replied that he had consumed no part of his living until he came into "the Kynges farvis," and added—"I parſeave you *Borne's* ſon of *Worſeter*, who was beholdon unto my uncle *Wynter*, and therfore you have no cauſe to be my enemy; nor yow never knew me, nor I yow before now, wich is too foone." "I have harde enough off yow," ſaid *Bourne*. "So have I off you," replied *Underhill*, "how that Mr. *Sheldone* drove you oute of *Worceterſhire* for your behavyoure." In the reign of *Elizabeth*, Sir *John Bourne*, being ſteward of the church of *Worceſter*, entered into great diſputes with the new Proteſtant Biſhop, *Edwin Sandys*, which led to various frays in *Worceſter*, and eventually to Sir *John's* impriſonment for ſix or ſeven weeks in the Marſhalſea, as narrated by *Strype*.

Another little illuſtration of the times may be found in the hiſtory of *Gilbert Bourne* (nephew of the outrageous Knight of *Holt* Caſtle and *Battenhall*, above-named), who was made one of the firſt Prebendaries of *Worceſter* in 1541. As he was preaching at St. *Paul's* in 1553, happening to obſerve that Biſhop *Bonner* was unjuſtly deprived, ſome of his audience became ſo offended that one of them fired a piſtol at him, and another threw a dagger which ſtuck in the pillar that ſupported the pulpit; thus evincing the popular opinion of the temporiſing policy both of *Bonner* and his advocate.

Elizabeth has been very juſtly accuſed of intolerance and persecution both by Papists and Puritans. On the one hand the oath of allegiance to Her Majesty was made a frightful bugbear, by which was incurred the forfeiture of all benefices and property, and even the punishment due to high treason was dealt out; while on the other the act of uniformity enforced the use of the *Book of Common Prayer*, on pain of perpetual imprisonment and heavy fines for every instance of non-attendance at the parish church. The "scavenger's daughter" plied her hateful trade as busily as, if there had been a Protestant inquisition, bending and compressing the bodies of wretched Catholics till blood issued from their ears and noses; iron gauntlets crushed their hands, needles were inserted under their nails, and many a poor recusant was introduced to the famous hole in the Tower known as "Little ease," where it was impossible to stand, sit, or lie. But our great maiden Queen is not altogether without excuse: she was beleaguered on all sides by powerful and designing enemies; and we who sit in easy arm chairs in these days of domestic peace and quietude know but little of the stern necessities which rendered strong measures essential to the policy of those times. *Pius V* had assumed to depose the Queen, and the Papal excommunication was posted by stealth on the Bishop of *London's* palace in the very heart of the metropolis. What with Catholic revolts and Proteſtant nonconformity—with rumours of plots and apprehenſions from Jeſuits—with the efforts made by *Spain* and other Catholic powers to coerce this kingdom in the matter of its religion—*Elizabeth's* bed was not one of roſes. Pope *Clement* uſed to vent his humour on Her Majeſty by calling her "an old woman without a huſband and without a certain ſucceſſor." His Holineſs might have been a little leſs bitter: *Elizabeth's* ſympathies were with Catholiciſm, but, true to her father's blood, ſhe could not tolerate a foreign Pope—at leaſt ſhe knew the nation would not again ſubmit to the yoke, and that her crown depended on her decided and vigorous ſupport of the cauſe of the Reformation. She tortured Catholics not ſo much for religion's ſake as on political grounds; and although the ſoundneſs of this policy may now be generally queſtioned—eſpecially as the bulk of the *Engliſh* Catholics repudiated the Pope's bull—it muſt be borne in mind that the age of *Elizabeth* had not arrived at a clear perception of the principles of conſtitutional liberty and religious toleration, while the nation had too much to dread from the ſtruggles and inſidious efforts of a powerful though fallen hierarchy to ceaſe for one moment from the moſt jealous watchfulneſs and repreſſive if not exterminating measures. One of the greatest objections to Catholicity was the Papal assumption of temporal power---an objection in which many influential *English* Catholics of that day seemingly concurred; and but for this development of the Papacy it is possible that even now the Western Church might have been undivided, though reformed.

In the month of May, 1559, mass was entirely abolished and images were generally destroyed. In the county of *Worcester*, I believe, only two sculptured figures now remain attached to churches, the survivors of the iconoclastic outbreak of that time---namely, at *Leigh* and *Rouselench*. All the Bishops, except *Anthony* of *Llandaff*, refused to take the oath of supremacy, and notwithstanding the vigilance with which the ports were guarded three of them escaped to the Continent, among them being Bishop *Richard Pate* of *Worcester*, who was succeeded by *Edward Sandys*. The parochial clergy, however, did not generally follow the example of their bishops, for out of 9,400 preferments, only 80 parish priests, 50 prebendaries, 15 heads of colleges, 12 archdeacons, 12 deans, 6 abbots, and the bishops, resigned their places; and of these self-denying few, I believe not one was an incumbent of any *Worcester* city parish, *Nash's* lists giving no presentation to any living in this city in 1559. The Catholic body now generally relinquished their old churches. For about fifteen years they had submitted to the Protestant laws of *Elizabeth*, and had attended the parish churches, under the idea that they had done quite enough if, in going and returning, they kept together and avoided the society of the Protestants. But now, a council declared the attendance at Protestant worship to be grievously sinful, and the payment of fines for absence from church was considered by far the lesser evil of the two. *Elizabeth* herself is said to have received 20,000*l.* a year from rich Catholics for dispensations not to attend Protestant worship; and although this is an allegation made by her enemies, Her Majesty's inherent and incurable acquisitiveness renders the truth of the charge not improbable.

The *English* mission of Jesuits was founded by Father *Persons* in 1572, and in the midland district the missioners laboured devotedly, but under great difficulties and in constant disguises. Then the proceedings against Catholics became more rigorous, priests being everywhere hunted up, imprisoned, expatriated, or executed; the rack and the gibbet groaned and creaked; every Catholic priest was ordered to quit the kingdom within forty days on pain of death, and those who gave aid or support to them were also condemned to death, just as if guilty of theft or murder. Parliament likewife granted power to Her Majefty to deftroy all priefts who, being exiled, fhould return to *England*, or who fhould dare to enter her dominions, fuch an act being declared high treafon. Neverthelefs, the laws neither prevented priefts from entering *England* nor the people from receiving and helping them. The fufferings which refulted herefrom may be gathered from the State trials, from documents ftill preferved at *Douay*, *Stoneyhurft*, &c., as alfo from the writings of Bifhop *Challoner*, Canon *Flanaghan*, and others. Of courfe at that time there was no public place of worfhip for the Catholics either at *Worcefter* or any other town in the kingdom, although the *Englifh* miffion had been confolidated in 1598 and the kingdom divided into twelve circuits, with a head prieft and chapter of twelve affiftants. In private houfes the rites of the *Romifh* faith were ftill celebrated; great care, however, was taken neither to admit many perfons at the fame moment nor to make the temporary chapel or abode of the prieft too confpicuous; for the prieft, hiding holes were prepared in gentlemen's houfes, of which numerous fpecimens ftill exift, as at *Coughton*, &c., while the place affigned for the mafs was ufually an obfcure room or garret, whither no one unobferved could go. This precaution was very neceffary, for prieft hunters abounded who laboured hard in their office in confequence of the reward of 100*l.* offered to every one who fhould convict a perfon of being a prieft. This grant was allowed as late even as 1778, and there are perfons ftill living who diftinctly remember going ftealthily to their garrets to hear mafs. Ordinarily the prieft had a home in fome nobleman's family, but did not remain long in one place, removing from one Catholic houfe to another, and from one county or diftrict to another, in various difguifes and under feigned names, encouraging his brethren in their day of trial and perfecution. At *Oxford*, in 1577, one *Roland Jenks*, a Catholic bookfeller, was condemned at the affizes to have his ears nailed to the pillory and to deliver himfelf when he felt inclined by tearing them off with his own hands; but no fooner was the fentence paffed than the judge, magiftrates, jury, and hundreds of others prefent, were ftruck with a ftrange mortal diftemper, which carried off many inftantly on the fpot and others foon afterwards. The Catholic chroniclers ufe this hiftorical fact as a divine interpofition in their favour, while others have feen in it only the neceffary refult of a neglect of fanitary precautions, combined with the extreme heat of the weather, the crowded ftate of the court, and the filthy condition of the prifoners.

The practice at that time was, when a prieft

was caught, to hang him, cut him down while alive, embowel and quarter the carcafe, and put up the four quarters on the gates or entrances to the town:

> " Indeed 't is true, and yet 't is wondrous odd,
> To hate each other for the love of GOD."

Before *Elizabeth's* death, fo long as there was a doubt of the fucceffion, *James* was lavifh of promifes to all parties, and among the reft to the afflicted Catholics; but when he afcended the throne, and petitions were prefented to him in favour of toleration, he difappointed both Puritans and Catholics, without earning the refpect of the Eftablifhed Church. Plots were then again rife, and the laws of *Elizabeth* were reimpofed with great rigour. In *Herefordfhire* efpecially it is ftated that 409 families were ftripped of everything in a very fhort time; and at *Warwick*, *John Sugar* was executed for being a feminary prieft. He was famous for his love of the poor, and had travelled on foot over a great part of *Worcefterfhire* and the adjoining counties. *Hindlip* Houfe, near *Worcefter*, was at an early period of the perfecution the great centre of Catholicity in this diftrict, whither high and low repaired, as is defcribed by *Juvency*, in his *Hiftoria Societatis Jefu*. This ancient manfion (fee frontifpiece) was then the refidence of Mr. *Habingdon*; and if in one retreat more than another great pains had been taken to afford shelter and safety to the hunted priests it was here. Mr. *Habingdon's* priest, *Edward Oldcorn* (a native of *York*), who had been stationed at *Hindlip* by his superior, *Garnett*, was long known as "the apostle of *Worcestershire*." His labours in this and the adjoining counties—the dangers he was exposed to and his miraculous escapes—are described as having been inconceivable. *Oliver*, in his *Collections*, says "It would require a volume to insert the good deeds of this virtuous, wise, and charitable father and indefatigable missioner—the number of persons whom he converted and of Catholics he reclaimed—of scholars whom he sent over to the seminaries, and of devout females to the convents." Father *Gerard* says, "Indeed I may safely say of him, without amplification, that *in illis partibus totas fere fundavit, rexitque ecclesias domesticas*. I neither do know nor have known any one priest in *England* that did go so many journeys as he did, especially towards the latter end of his time, when he grew to be acquainted with so many places that he could never almost stay three days at home but he should be sent for." *Thomas Lister*, another Jesuit, also resided at *Hindlip* with *Oldcorn*, as stated in *Gerard's* MS.: "*Habebat autem socium insignem et doctum patrem Thomam Listerum.*" Here also was *Ralph*

Ashley (alias Chambers), a lay brother and the attached servant of *Oldcorn*.

The circumstances of the Gunpowder Plot are no doubt well known to my readers, and the connection therewith of several *Worcestershire* families—*Winter* of *Huddington*, *Lyttelton* of *Hagley*, and *Habingdon* of *Hindlip*. *Catesby* and *Percy*, the principal conspirators, with their followers, took shelter in a house of *Lyttelton's* at *Holbeach*, but being attacked by the High Sheriff of *Worcestershire*, were slain with some others, and the rest ultimately taken—*Winter* at *Hagley*, and *Lyttelton* at *Prestwood*. *Garnett*, suspected of having been privy to the plot, was fain to seek concealment; and being invited to *Hindlip* by *Oldcorn*, he took shelter there. But *Lyttelton*, who was tried at *Worcester*, and condemned for treason because he had received *Winter* into his house, gave information (with the view of obtaining a pardon for himself) of the hiding places of the two Jesuits and their followers at *Hindlip*. The circumstances of the retreat, the search, capture, and subsequent treatment of these men, must now be given in a manner probably new to my readers, who have been accustomed to view this matter entirely from a Protestant point of view. Let us hear what Father *Juvency* has to say on this subject, premising that my extract is a liberal translation from the *Latin*:

"Being thus ejected from the station which he had long occupied, he *(Garnett)* was invited by *Oldcorn* to the house of the *Habingdons*, where *Oldcorn* himself had lived a long time. The house or castle was a large one, situated at about the third mile stone from *Worcester*, and was called *Henlip;* it had various parts connected together by passages, so that you might call it a labyrinth; and when the examiners came to find out priests they went away, tired out by the inextricable mazes of the recesses or hiding places. In this castle, as in a strong citadel, *Oldcorn* preserved the Catholic religion for sixteen years, and they used commonly to call him *Hall*, under which name, as if a kinsman of *Habingdon's*, he was known and beloved not only by Catholics but also by the very heretics themselves, on account of his very bland manners; and hither from the whole province congregated for the sake of piety the Catholic nobility, who used to join *Oldcorn* in the sacraments and other ordinances of the church. There often, with others, had been *Humphrey Littleton*, who was detected in having received the conspirators (who soon after the conspiracy had fled from the city) into his own house. Having been thrown into prison on that account, and sentenced to death, he unhappily thought it might procure his pardon if he indicated the hiding place of the fathers. Accordingly he named the house of Mr. *Habingdon*, where he divulged that *Garnett* was living with *Oldcorn*.

"Exulting in an incredible manner at this information, *H. Bromley*---by far the most impure of the Puritans---flies off with 200 horsemen, having been set over this business by Parliament, and with the hope of grasping his *(Habingdon's)* estate, which was contiguous to his own. He surrounds the castle with part of his attendants, some of whom he leads to the gates, which not being opened as soon as usual on such occasions, he breaks down the door, and passing through the breach he receives the keys of the house, and garrisons every part, just as in a surrendered city. Having examined every part of it for eight days, but being unable by any art to find out the blind entrances and the hiding places, he determined at last to keep a watch until hunger should wear out those who were concealed, and force them to surrender. Nor was success wanting to his design, for two men servants (*Owen* and *Ashley*) almost dead with hunger* and desirous to consult the interest of the fathers, who they saw would perish in a short time for want of food, emerged from their retreat, and being immediately seized, they represented themselves as being *Oldcorn* and *Garnett*, expecting to be at once carried off---in which case the fathers could have escaped---but a light having been brought, and they being closely inspected, and persons being called who knew both the priests, the fraud was detected, and the search was renewed. Some days were consumed in overhauling the walls, in breaking the floors and wainscots, and opening the ceilings. At length they found their prey in a recess in the

* The two servants had but one apple to subsist upon for three days; the two fathers had been maintained by means of a quill or reed passed through a hole into the gentlewomen's chamber, by which broths and soups were sucked in.

upper ceiling, which had been elegantly painted over, and the difcovery well repaid the labour. Shouts followed the fuccefsful difcovery, and a frefh party having come from *London*, *Garnett* and *Oldcorn* were carried back in triumph in the midft of them, although it was in reality a triumph of patience, moderation, and charity--- through the odour of which virtues, by degrees *Bromley* (and others who had joined themfelves as companions to *Bromley* for the fake of honour) began to fpeak highly of *Garnett*, efpecially of his doctrine, piety, and moderation.

" Three days after, when firft brought out of prifon, they followed him with an unufual demonftration of honour, and the judges were fo foftened by his firft anfwers that one of them did not hefitate to fay openly there could be nothing in the character and caufe of fo excellent a man, except his Papiftical doctrine, that he *(Garnett)* fhould dread feverity in his judgment. But a method and a colour of accufation was to be fought which was to deftroy *Garnett* in the name of a confpiracy. This pretext was not found till after four months.

" The caufe of *Oldcorn* was decided firft, and three things were objected againft him, firft, that he had invited *Garnett* to *Henlip;* fecond, that he had recommended by letter to Father *Jones* to hide two of the confpirators; and third, that he had appeared to approve of the confpiracy by his anfwers. One witnefs *(H. Littleton)* was induced to accufe him, in the hope of obtaining a pardon for himfelf. *Oldcorn* admitted that he had invited *Garnett* to a hiding place at *Henlip*, but that was before it had been forbidden by edict; as to the second charge, he denied having written letters to *Jones*; and on the third, he admitted having spoken to *Littleton* about the conspiracy, but not approving of it. These answers did not satisfy the judges, who in vain endeavoured by torture to draw out further admissions, and at length they declared that so far as he had spoken out he appeared to be innocent, but by what he had concealed in his mind he was guilty! * * *

" The conspirators were so worn out by torture that they could scarcely advance a step. *Oldcorn* himself, who should have been treated more mildly, as being only suspected by the lightest conjecture, in the hearing of all the people affirmed that he was five times tortured, and once for five hours so dreadfully that his mind and almost his life failed him. To which attestation none of the judges present opposed anything, or it would have been abundantly refuted by the silent aspect of *Oldcorn* himself; his loosened arms and hands sufficiently confirmed this impious cruelty. In consequence of this he was unable to subscribe his name to the savage sentence, and the officer of the court inserted the pen between his deadened fingers, drew his languid hand, and marked out some straggling words. The judges seemed now deterred by shame, and several *London* lawyers argued against the iniquity of the proceedings. *Oldcorn* was then removed to *Worcester*, so that he might perish more obscurely. *Habingdon* and *Winter* were also led with him, and *Littleton* was sentenced to die with them. When he saw that he had been deceived with the hope of life he openly confessed his treason, and declared that he died deservedly because he had been the means of putting *Oldcorn* and *Garnett* to death, and from *Oldcorn* he supplicated pardon for his falsehood, publicly detesting his perfidy. Not only this penitence of a Catholic man affected *Oldcorn* with great comfort, but also the sudden conversion of a Calvinistic young man (almost lost) who came over to the better part; for the latter, being in the same prison with *Oldcorn*, and being about to suffer the punishment due to his wickedness the day after, relying on the vain doctrine of *Calvin*---that faith in *Christ* alone expunged all our sins, so that we need not fear danger or destruction after death---relying on that vain faith, the young man laughed at the Catholics piously preparing themselves for death, while he kept dancing and singing all night. But *Oldcorn* addressing himself to him in his bland manner, after earnest prayers to *God*, taught him good things, and brought him to a detestation of his wickedness; he was reconciled to the church, cast away his errors, and took the benefit of confession.

" Joyful in this victory, *Oldcorn* proceeded to the scene of punishment, or rather of glory, on the 7th of April; and when he came within sight of the people, with a loud voice he called *God* to witness that death was brought on him for two reasons, first, because he had exercised the office of a priest; and second, because he had received *Garnett*, although he had not then been proscribed by edict. Being then interrogated by the magistrate why he was silent about the third and principal charge, namely the conspiracy, he replied that this charge could not pertain to him as he had never said or done anything in consequence of which he should be considered deservedly guilty of the conspiracy. After these things, having piously called on *God*, he gave himself up to the hangman, by whom he was suspended and cut open; his heart and intestines, according to custom, were thrown into the fire, and from the place where his remains were buried flames broke out for sixteen days, which a copious rain was not able to extinguish. *Worcester* ran together as if to a portent; and the magistrate, seeing his own iniquity shine out by the flames, did not cease till he had entirely covered them with mould after the fashion of a mountain.* But he did not on that account succeed in burying the memory of this excellent man. Indeed *Worcester* used to look upon him as her own apostle. To him, as to an oracle, all Catholics used to apply, by whose wisdom they might be ruled, and by whose charity they might be cherished. Both laymen and priests, tossed about by the wild waves of that troublous time, used to come together to the house of *Habingdon* as to a safe harbour. He added many to the Catholic ranks, and saved from heresy *Dorothy*, the sister of *Habingdon*. Scarcely anything shows more clearly either the admirable power of grace or the excellence of *Oldcorn* than the conversion of this lady. She had grown up in the court of *Elizabeth*, almost in the bosom of heresy, nor did she merely oppose the Catholic disputants pertinaciously after the manner of women, but as was thought she answered sagaciously and very

---

* The bailiffs for *Worcester* in 1605-6 were *Thomas Chetle* and *Edward Mitton.*

theologically. *Oldcorn* seemed a most suitable man either to oppose the female spirit by his erudition or soften it by his politeness and polished manner. His first labour was in vain: if she found herself unable to repel the weapons of reason by force she eluded them by craft, and broke them by a persistency always unconquered, being indeed ashamed to confess herself overcome. What could *Oldcorn* do? The voice of *Christ* speaking came to his mind, that this was a certain kind of demon, which could not be driven out of her except by prayer and fasting. The disputation being left off, he engages in prayer and preserved a four days' fast. For the first two days, *Dorothy*, wondering that he did not eat, suspected that he was very ill, and finding that he abstained from all food for a third and even a fourth day, she inquired the cause. This being made known to her, looking at the great charity of the man, and being moved by Divine inspiration, she threw herself at his feet: being before arrogantly pretentious, she is now modest and humble; from being a mistress of error, she is now a disciple of the truth.

" *Oldcorn* had been at *Henlip* for sixteen years, being often protected by the manifest interposition of *God* from plots to discover him. On one occasion, *Bromley*, being informed that he was within, came quietly with a body of men, and having scaled the wall, descended into the garden where *Oldcorn* was by chance taking his exercise. The party civilly saluted him (not knowing it was *Oldcorn*) and passed by, when he immediately slipped away into his hiding place. Having made a long and fruitless search, a suspicion crossed their minds that he was the very man of whom they were in search, but running back, they found he was gone; and their belief that he had escaped by flight was confirmed on finding that a horse which they had at first seen in the stable had also disappeared. Being uncertain which way he had fled, they at that time abandoned the search. A horse was afterwards found feeding in a neighbouring meadow, but no one could ascertain by whom it had been led there or by which gate it had gone out. The searchers, however, did not so soon go away, for they were satisfied by certain proofs that *Oldcorn* was lying hid there; so they surrounded the house with a circle of men, and for three days and nights tore the walls to pieces, digging through in more than twenty places. At last they came to a wall in which he was hidden; they beat the stones one by one with hammers, partly to move them and partly to try the sound, for if a harsh or dull sound was returned it would give proof of some hollow. At each of the blows, *Oldcorn* made the sign of the cross, by which the stones were so guarded as to give back only a solid and clear sound, seeming harder than adamant. The search was, therefore, abandoned, and the men went away tired. Nor did the powers above take less care of *Oldcorn* when he was induced to wander out of that castle whither the salvation of souls invited him. Having with some companions entered on a journey by night he was seized by a troop of watchmen and carried before a neighbouring justice, by whom he is asked who he is, and why travelling in those parts at that unseasonable time. But behold there suddenly stood by him an old man unknown, who pleaded for him in so apposite an oration that he quite satisfied the justice. He is, therefore, dismissed with the appearance of honour, without having his baggage examined, in which, if the furniture of sacred service and the books of a priest had been found, he could not have escaped being discovered and condemned without delay.

"In this manner the powers above, being present, guarded his life, as before that they had taken care of his health by a singular benefit; for when he was constantly emaciating himself by voluntary penances --- in which thing holy persons scarce keep safe bounds --- having burst a vein in his chest, he poured out a great quantity of blood, so that he often lay destitute of strength and half dead. In addition to this there was a putrid ulcer in his mouth, and an incurable cancer. He, however, undertook a pilgrimage to St. *Winifred's* shrine, which is situated in *Wales*, and returned free from both diseases."

Challoner states that *Oldcorn*, on his way to the well, lodged at a Catholic house, and was told by the priest of the family that a stone which had been taken out of the aforesaid well was kept in the house. *Oldcorn*, after the mass, applied this stone to his mouth, devoutly recommending himself to the prayers of St. *Winifred*, and in half an hour was perfectly cured of his cancer. St. *Winifred's* well was in great esteem among the *Worcestershire* Catholics. Jesuit *Owen* reports the cure of *Roger Whetston,* then about sixty years of age, of an inveterate lameness by drinking the water of this well, on 28th August, 1667. This poor man came from *Bromsgrove,* and from having been a " Quaker and Anabaptist " is said to have become a serious Catholic, and his son, then about eleven years of age, was christened *Catholico more,* unto whom the greatest persons in the country were pleased to be patrines."

For the extraordinary circumstances attending the execution of *Oldcorn* I have consulted *More's History of the Anglican Mission,* of whose narrative the following is a rough translation:

"*Oldcorn* being sent back to *Worcester,* to await the sentence of the accustomed local tribunals, he was there shut up in custody with common malefactors, and the day before he was led to his trial he had a companion in his chains, namely, a very wicked robber, charged with many crimes; who, although he was to meet his punishment the day after, seemed free from care, and wandered about the prison leisurely employing himself in dancing, singing, and jokes, sometimes addressing one and then another with his facetiæ, and rallying Father *Oldcorn* on the superfluous anxiety which seemed to be consuming him before the time. The father, prudently thinking that the salvation of his companion was rather to be considered than his own continued communication with *God,* addressed the man, and asked wherein was the ground or cause of his trust. If he felt no fear as to the next world, because he thought there was nothing there either to be feared or hoped for, such a sentiment was unworthy of a Christian; but if he feared not on account of the merits of *Christ*, which are our only ground of trust, he ought to remember that not faith only but good works were required of us by *Christ*. The most certain way to confidence was this: to unite to the merits of *Christ* our obedience to his precepts. The robber (after more argument of this kind) entirely and thoughtfully delivered himself up to the instructor; the rest of the day was spent in instruction and the night in confession. The next day, when both were being led to the place of execution, this man, separating himself from the other convicts, followed behind the hurdle on which the father was being dragged through kennels filthy with mire. Being asked why he did so, he said, 'I follow my father, who showed me the way of salvation, for in the faith which he professes I have determined to die.' 'Are you' (they say) 'a Papist rogue?' Said he, 'I was a thief, I confess, and a robber, while I was yours; but now, by the mercy of *God* and the assistance of this man, I have become a Catholic, and am doing the penance of sinners with a firm hope of eternal life.'

"In one day, therefore, three were carried off by a similar punishment---being partners in one faith and one reward---namely, *Oldcorn*, and the robber, and *Rodolph (Ashley)*, the servant of *Oldcorn*. This man and *John Owen* (whom we have mentioned), on the tenth day after they had hidden themselves, came out, either forced by want of food or induced by hope (as sometimes happens) that they would be feized in miftake for the priefts; but *Garnett* was too well known for the obfervers to be deceived by the appearance of another. Therefore *Rodolph* was punifhed fimply for having been the fervant of a prieft. As foon as *Oldcorn* reached the firft ftep of the ladder on which he was mounting, *Rodolph* coming up impreffed a kifs on the footftep, faying, 'O happy man that I am, who have been given as fervant to this faint, and by him brought to live well, and now about to make an end of life by fo bleffed a death.' ('He met his death,' fays *Oliver*, 'with the tranquillity and fortitude becoming the difciple of fuch a friend and father.') The body of *Oldcorn* having been cut into four parts, the bowels were thrown into a ditch, and are faid to have burnt with fire for fixteen days---about the fame number as the years in which he, while living, had ftriven to communicate the Divine fire to the minds of the men of that region. This is confidered to have been a prodigy, efpecially as a copious rain had fallen during that time. On the feventeenth day the people collecting from the neighbouring places much earth was thrown on the flames, which were with difficulty extinguifhed.

"And another thing is related to illuftrate the memory of both (*Oldcorn* and *Garnett*). There is before the houfe of *Habingdon* a large court, bounded by a wall; there, after the two captives had been led out and mounted on horfeback, their laft footftep appeared clothed with a new kind of grafs, fuch as had never been feen by any one before that day---and not rifing up confufedly and without order, but which imitated the figure of an imperial crown, the herbage coming together in a heap; and although the doors had been thrown down by the force and preffure of the party firft rufhing in, whereby there lay open an accefs for animals of any kind, while they fed on the reft they ufed to leave that untouched. Thefe may be confidered trifling circumftances, and capable of various interpretations, yet *God* not unfrequently fpeaks by trifling things of this kind, in the fame manner as by the ivy of *Iona* and the unfruitful fig-tree, and thus calls us to higher things. And as the difciples and others varioufly interpreted the parables fpoken by *Chrift*, fo if any one think that the innocence of thefe men and their holinefs of life is confirmed by thefe proofs he is by no means to be oppofed, fince he does not depart from the cuftom of *Chrift* and his difciples in parables."

Challoner gives further particulars of *Oldcorn's* trial and execution, from which it appears that the trial took place at *Worcefter* Lenten Affize, and the execution on April 7th, 1606, being the Monday in Paffion Week, at Red Hill, near *Worcefter*, on the *London* Road. He was hung, cut down, and butchered alive at the age of forty-five; his head and quarters were fet upon poles in different parts of the city, and his heart and bowels caft into the fire, which (*Challoner* adds) continued to fend forth a lively flame for fixteen days. A fonnet was compofed on this execution, of which the following is a fample:

"Few words he spoke; they stopped his mouth,
And choked him with a cord;
And left he should be dead too soon,
No mercy they afford;
But quick and live they cut him down,
And butcher him full soon,
Behead, tear, and dismember straight,
And laugh when all was done."

Oliver remarks---

" I hope in *God* the time will come when the city of *Worcester* shall see and acknowledge both the burning charity with which Father *Oldcorn* lived and died among them, and the crown of glory he hath received of the hand of *God* for his faith so truly kept and his course so happily consummated. His life was holy, his death saintly. *God* send us part of his blessed merits and intercession."

Littleton was also executed at the same time, together with *John Winter*, *Perks* of *Hagley*, and *Burford* his man, for receiving and entertaining *Robert Winter* and *S. Littleton* at the time of their flight, contrary to the King's proclamation. *Garnett* met his fate in St. *Paul's* Churchyard, *London*, on the 3rd of May, 1606; and the Catholic historians declare that some drops of blood falling from his head on a stalk of straw arranged themselves into a minute but distinct resemblance of Father *Garnett*, the features, beard, and neck, being all exactly formed to his likeness. This straw was said to have been at *Stoneyhurst* College for years, and Father *Richard*

Blount avouches the truth of the tale, "for," says he, "besides ourselves, a thousand others are witnesses of it."* Moreover, *Garnett's* head being placed on *London* Bridge, is said to have "retained the same lively colour for which it had been conspicuous during life for about twenty days, which drew all *London* to the spectacle." The servant man *Owen*, above mentioned, had also an *alias*, namely "Little *John*," and is said to have possessed wonderful ingenuity in contriving secret places for priests to hide in, besides extraordinary discretion and judgment, so that he maintained the unbounded esteem and confidence of the Catholic clergy and gentry; he was put on the rack for seven hours together in the Tower of *London*, but never divulged his secrets; and they tortured him "till his bowels and his life gushed out together."

My readers may attach what weight they choose to the above-mentioned evidence of miracles, by which the ecclesiastics of those days

---

* In a tract called *The Fiery Trial*, published in *London*, 1612, the author, in an account of Popish miracles, says, "Adde hereto also their late coyned woonder of *Garnet's* face in a wheat strawe: *vide librum cuius tituli pars est, vera historia de admirabili spica.* Rightly Englished---

"' A fabulous story of a fained straw
First divulged by a foolish jack-dawe.'"

For a copy of the above, with many other scarce and valuable works, now in the *Worcester* Cathedral Library, I am indebted to the kindness of the Very Rev. the Dean.

maintained their hold upon the superstitious masses; but it should be borne in mind that the works from which I have quoted were published at a sufficient distance from the scene of supernatural appearances, and in a language unknown to the mass of the people, so that no fear could be apprehended of an examination into or contradiction of the alleged facts. The remembrance of the Gunpowder Plot was long kept up in *Worcestershire* with probably greater animus against Popery than in most other counties, owing to the local incidents which have been already detailed. On every recurring 5th of November the *Worcester* Corporation provided fuel for the bonfires and drink for the happy spectators, who paraded their "*Guy*" and committed him to the flames with that intense satisfaction which usually accompanies an act of religious patriotism. The wood and thatch of those days, however, did not suit the development of bonfires, and after many ruinous conflagrations had occured in the city, this popular demonstration against Popery was cried down in 1789, but still lingers amongst us in the shape of an occasional squib or a cracker discharged by some enterprising youth when P. C. has turned the corner.

Robert North, alias *Duckett*, another Jesuit, is mentioned by *Gerard*, in his *Latin* Autobiography, as having been a prisoner in *Worcester*

Gaol when *Oldcorn* was executed; he, however, got free from the toils, and was living at *St. Omer's* in 1609. *John Floyd,* alfo a Jefuit in the Englifh miffion, in attempting to penetrate to *Oldcorn,* while the latter was detained a clofe prifoner in *Worcefter* Gaol, was apprehended and lay in prifon for a year, when he was fentenced to perpetual banifhment. *More* fays of him—

" *John,* the brother of *Henry Floyd,* learnt by experience that everything is not fafe which appears fo, for going to fee our *Oldcorn* in *Worcefter* Gaol he was detained there, and neither by entreaty nor the offer of a ranfom was he able to obtain his liberation, *Popham* being an obftacle.* After a year's exile he went to *St. Omer's* and devoted four years to preaching and bringing to light the various errors of the heretics, with great applaufe both for ingenuity and doctrine. Then returning to *England,* he was often bought off from the purfuivants, and at length emigrated to *Louvain.*"

In Father *Perfons's Judgment of a Catholic Englifhman,* publifhed in 1608, he fays that " no night paffed comonly but that foldiours and

* *Popham* was Attorney General in 1582-3, and Chief Juftice in 1601; and concerning him and others, whofe families were enriched by abbey lands, in "the weft countrie," the old couplet may here be quoted:

" *Popham, Horner,* and *Thynne,*
When the monks popped out they popp'd in."

catchpoles brake into quiet men's houses when they were asleep, and not onlye carryed awaye their persons into prisons, at their pleasure, except they would brybe themselves excessively, but whatever lyked them best besydes in the house, eyther of bookes, cuppes, chalyces, or other furniture that might anywayes seeme or be apprehended to belong to religion, was taken for a prey and seized on;" and he mentions a Mrs. *Shelley*, "a gentlewoman of good worshippe, being caste into the common jayle at *Worcester*, for that the priest, *M. Hassells*, was found in her house."

Churchwardens and constables were now ordered to present, at Sessions once a year, the names of all Catholics, their children and servants; and any Catholic once convicted of not attending the parish church was to forfeit 20*l.* a month for his whole life, and the King was empowered to seize two-thirds of his property; every Catholic was also forbidden to go more than five miles from his house without permission of a Justice or a Bishop. The oath of allegiance and supremacy was tendered to all suspected residents and travellers, and if they refused to take it the consequence was imprisonment and præmunire. One ray of sunshine was shed on the poor Catholics when *James* was endeavouring to secure for his son *Charles* the hand of the *Spanish*

Infanta, the *Spaniards* demanding as a provifo to the marriage that the penal laws fhould not be enforced; but when the match was broken off, the laws were again let loofe. *Charles*, however, married another Catholic lady—*Henrietta* of *France*, and then as much toleration as the *Englifh* Parliament and people would permit was allowed. At that time there were five Jefuit miffioners in the *Worcefterfhire* diftrict.

In 1622, Father *Blount*, then Vice-Provincial, erected Jefuits' Colleges in *England*, including, foon after, that of *St George's* for *Worcefter* and *Warwick*. In 1623, *England* was erected into a province, and Father *Blount* was appointed Firft Provincial. *Worcefter*, I believe, was called a "refidence," being a ftation over which there was no fuperior, the miffioner at a refidence differing in this refpect from the miffioner at a college, who had a local fuperior. Thefe refidences had not neceffarily the means of fupport within themfelves, but their independence of a local rector was the great diftinction of, and gave importance to, the refidence.

Father *Anderfon* (from *Norfolk*) laboured in this miffion with great fuccefs, and was inftrumental in the converfion of the daughter of the Bifhop of *Worcefter*,* about the year 1630.

* Bifhop *John Thornborough*, who is defcribed as an accomplifhed man, and a writer on the philofopher's ftone.

More, in his *Latin* history previously quoted, gives an interesting account of the circumstances of this Bishop's family:

"The then false Bishop of *Worcester* had a large offspring, which he had taken care to bring up diligently from their cradles in the same heresy as himself; but indeed by the goodness of *God*, one of his daughters having embraced the Catholic faith, was an example to many of piety and constancy. Her eldest brother---a man immersed in the filth of all wickedness---had come to extremities, from the effects of a dangerous disease; and being touched by either true or feigned religious motives, spoke to his sister, who was anxious about his health, and besought her more than once that she would send for a priest, he vehemently asserting that he desired to die as a Catholic. Accordingly, lest so necessary a thing should be wanting to her brother in his danger, she called one of our priests, who having received the confession of a whole life, refreshed the sick man with the heavenly bread; a second time he returned to strengthen the neophyte by the same sacraments. He is asked a third time to come; but in the meantime the unhappy man had discovered to his parent what had been going on. A snare was laid, and the priest (*William Anderson*), was caught. On being brought before the Bishop, and an oath which they called the 'oath of fidelity' being refused, he was put into close confinement (in a loathsome dungeon). Meanwhile the sick man, like a wretched deserter, soon suffered a most unhappy death, being never heard to name *God* except when he violated that moſt ſacred name by his ſacrilegious oaths, but uſed to cry out that an evil devil was ſtanding by him with horrid form and aſpect, and he alſo heard the prieſt upbraiding him with his wickedneſs and the injury he had done him. The prieſt being removed to *London*, at length by favour of the Queen obtaining his freedom, he ſpent ſome more years in the ſame work, and cloſed his days (1657) at *St. Omer's*, where he had received his early education."

About the year 1630, Father *Edward Siliſdon* aſſiſted in the Catholic miſſion at *Worceſter*. He was born in *Suffolk* in 1594, and became ſuperior of the *Worceſterſhire* miſſion; *obiit* January 3, 1659. There were ſaid to be not leſs than one thouſand miſſionaries in *England* in the year 1634, and as they died their places were readily ſupplied from foreign colleges eſtabliſhed for the purpoſe. In the laſt-named year, *Edward Knott* publiſhed at *St. Omer's* a work entitled *Mercy and Truth, or Charity maintained by Catholics; by way of Reply upon an Anſwer lately framed by Dr. Potter, Dean of Worceſter, to a Treatiſe which had formerly proved that Charity was miſtaken by Proteſtants, with the want whereof Catholics are unjuſtly charged for affirming that Proteſtancy unrepented deſtroys ſalvation*. The national jealouſy againſt Popery was now greatly on the increaſe, and in the *Townſend* MSS. is a parliamentary order, signed, "*Littilton,*" London, 18th November, 1641, to the following effect:

"To his loving friends, the Sheriff, Deputy-Lieutenants, and Justices of the Peace within the County of *Worcester*: Whereas there hath notice been given to the Parliament that the Popish recusants have appointed a day to assemble themselves, being the 18th day of this instant November, within certain counties of this kingdom, whereof your county is one, which may tend to the great disturbance of the peace of this kingdom, these are, therefore, in His Majesty's name and by authority of Parliament to will and require you, the Sheriffs and Deputy-Lieutenants, Justices of the Peace, and all other officers of the several counties, to look carefully that no such unlawful assemblies shall be; and to require you to suppress such assemblies or meetings by the force of the countie or otherwise, as you will answer it to the contrary."

In August, 1642, the *Worcester* County Grand Jury made a declaration to defend the Protestant religion against Popish recusants and others; and in the following month the trained soldiers and commoners of the city entreated the mayor and chamber "to take order that no Papists or recusants be suffered to take houses nor be resident within the city;" in obedience to which request Mr. Mayor granted "that the Lord *Lovelace* and one Mr. *Stanford,* who are by the commons declared to be delinquents and Papists, should be required speedily to depart the city; and if they do not upon such request depart, they shall by lawful means be enforced thereunto."

When the Puritans prevailed in Parliament, at the period verging on the Commonwealth, all sects united in denouncing the Catholics. In 1643, sequestrators were appointed for the several counties, whose duty was, among others, to seize and confiscate two parts out of three of the estates of all Papists, for the use of the Parliament; and the State Paper Office contains several hundred volumes of names of the sufferers. Presbyterian services now supplanted those of the Anglican Church, and for some years that party shared with the Independents and Baptists the use of our cathedrals and parish churches, where their sermons were regulated by the hour glass, relics of which still remain at *Shelsley* and elsewhere in this county. More and more severe were now the persecutions of the Catholics, and intense the feeling excited against them. Dr. *Prattenton*, in his MS. collections for *Worcestershire*, quotes a diary in which it is said that *Charles Price*, who had been an active man in raising forces for the King in *Wales*, was stabbed at *Worcester*, January 30, 1645, " for showing some discontent that Papists were received into greatest favour and Protestants thrust out of office." And in December of the same year a Proteftant affociation which had been formed in the north-weft part of the county of *Worcefter* among other regulations directed " that in all our meetings and general rendezvous all Papifts, or other perfons adhering to or holding intelligence with Papifts, be excluded the field and lift of our communication; and if they or any of them fhall offer to intrude on our affemblies at fuch meetings, and after warning given will not feverally depart, that then they fhall be difarmed, and the arms fo taken from them fhall be delivered to the conftable of each particular parifh refpectively where fuch perfon fo difarmed doth dwell, to be kept for His Majefty's fervice when occafion fhall be to make ufe of them. And no Papifts, or others holding intelligence with them, to receive the benefit of public protection. All foldiers to be firft billeted at their houfes, and no horfes or teams to be taken till all theirs are gone; and all fuch perfons are to be impreffed into His Majefty's fervice fo far as defirable." *Cromwell* ordered all priefts to quit the kingdom on pain of death, and all Cavaliers and Catholics were to go twenty miles from the metropolis. The Protector alfo placed over the militia diftricts officers (Major General *Berry* being affigned to the counties of *Worcefter*, *Hereford*, *Salop*, and *North Wales*) who, among other things, were to take care that

Papists and disaffected persons should be deprived
of their arms; the principal allegation then
made against the Catholics being, that they had
arrayed themselves under the unfortunate banner
of the miserable *Stuarts*—an act which was
rewarded by the second *Charles*, when he came
to the throne, by ordering all Jesuits and priests
to quit the kingdom. Nevertheless, that notable
monarch was wont to say that " the only religion
for a *gentleman* was Catholicism "—an opinion
he had probably arrived at from the circum-
stance that although he had fallen into the hands
of about ninety Catholics in succession after his
fatal defeat at *Worcester* he was not betrayed by
any one of them; and when the circumstances
of his death are taken into account, it will be
readily believed that his lack of toleration for
the Catholics was occasioned more by the " pres-
sure from without " than by any other cause, it
seeming extremely improbable that he possessed
a true regard for any form of religion, but only
that kind of distant respect for Catholicism which
should " make his mind easy " in his latter mo-
ments. The growth of Popery during this reign,
however, was so apparent, notwithstanding the
great fire of *London* had raised a loud outcry against
Catholics, that the House of Commons, in an
address to the throne in 1670, complained among
other things that " the Papists in *Yorkshire* com-

monly rang a bell to call the people to mafs." Still no public chapels had yet ventured to make their appearance: the Mitre Tavern at *Oxford*, and private houfes at *Worcefter*, *Wolverhampton*, and other places, were then ufed regularly for mafs; and at the *Coombe*, in *Herefordfhire*, was a fraternity of Popifh priefts.

The utmoft vigilance was, however, ufed at this period by the Proteftants, both in Church and State, to unmafk their religious opponents, an inftance of which is fhown in the articles of vifitation exhibited to minifters, churchwardens, &c., in 1662, one of the inquiries put to thofe officers being the following: "Are there any convicted Papifts, known Anabaptifts, Familifts, Quakers, and other feparatifts, in your parifh?"

In the year 1678, Father *Befwick*, *alias Sanders*, was prieft at *Worcefter*, and after thirty-two years of miffionary labour he died here in March, 1680, at the age of fixty-one.

Titus Oates's famous difcovery of a plot to eftablifh the Pope in the government of this country was no doubt an impudent fiction at the expenfe of the Catholics, defigned to work up the nation into fury. Oates himfelf was a fingular exemplification of the mutability of human fortunes: penfioned by *Charles II* with 1,200*l*. a year, he was imprifoned, whipped, and pilloried by *James*, awarded the more moderate allowance of 400*l.* per annum by "the deteſtable Dutchman," as *William III* has been denominated, and finally died at an advanced age. His pretended diſcloſures had the effect of hurrying a multitude of Catholics to priſon and the ſcaffold. Prieſts were again executed for the mere fact of being prieſts, as was the caſe with Father *Wall*, a Franciſcan, who was put to death at *Worceſter*, and his body laid in St. *Oſwald's* burying-ground, Auguſt 22, 1679, the ſame day on which Father *Kemble*, or *Campbell*, ſuffered in a ſimilar manner at *Hereford*.

From a narrative written by himſelf, and preſerved among the records of the *Engliſh* Franciſcans at *Douay*, it appears that *John Wall*, alias *Francis Johnſon*, was born of a good family in *Lancaſhire*, in 1620, had a good eſtate of 500*l.* a year, which he abandoned for the ſake of religion; ſtudied at the *Engliſh* College of *Douay*, and at thirty-two years of age took the habit of St. *Francis*. In 1656 he was ſent to the *Engliſh* miſſion, his reſidence being in *Worceſterſhire*, where he was ſometime known by the name of *Webb*, and was eſteemed a laborious miſſioner. He was in *London* when the King's proclamation came forth (after *Titus Oates's* plot), commanding all Catholics to depart from thence by the Friday following; he obeyed, and came to a friend's houſe in *Worceſterſhire*, not intending to ſtay there;

but the King's second proclamation being presently published, that no Catholic should walk above five miles without being stopped and carried before a Justice to have the oaths tendered, he took counsel of both Protestants and Catholics, and concluded it wiser to stay. The Sheriff's deputy came to the house where he was, with six or eight men, to arrest a gentleman for debt, and not finding him, broke down the doors, and among them the unfortunate priest's, before he was out of bed, and by mistake arrested him. On being taken before a Justice, the wife of the latter had a private interview with the prisoner, using her best persuasion to make him take the oaths; but he, thanking her, said he was not moved by fear or danger. Subsequently he was taken before Sir *John Pakington*, who asked him who he was, to which he replied that he had been in *Worcestershire* for twenty years and was well known; he declined to take the oaths, though he declared that he ever had been and would be a good subject. Sir *John Pakington* and Mr. *Townsend* committed him (Dec., 1678) for trial, previous to which he was in *Worcester* Castle (the old gaol) for five months. What he suffered here, and with what disposition of mind, may be gathered best from his own words:

"Imprisonment (says he) in these times especially, when none can fend to their friends, nor friends come to them, is the beft means to teach us how to put our confidence in *God* alone in all things ; and then He will make His promife good, that all things shall be added to us (*Luke* xii) ; which chapter, if every one would read and make good use of, a prifon would be better than a palace, and a confinement for religion and a good confcience fake more pleafant than all the liberties the world could afford."

He was brought upon his trial at *Worcefter*, April 25, 1679, before Judge *Atkins*, upon an indictment of high treason, for being a prieft and remaining in this realm contrary to the ftatute of *Elizabeth* 27. He would neither confefs nor deny his priefthood, but defended himfelf very prudently. There was only one witnefs that voluntarily appeared againft him (*Rogers* by name, who did fo for lucre fake, and who fwore that he had received the facrament at the prieft's hands, although it was fhown that he had never feen the prieft till the latter was in gaol), and three others that came by compulfion ; however, the jury found him guilty of the indictment, and the Judge pronounced fentence againft him in the ufual form, as in cafes of high treafon. Upon which the prieft made a bow, and faid aloud, " Thanks be to *God*; *God* fave the King ; and I befeech *God* to blefs your Lordfhip and all this honourable Bench." The Judge replied, " You have spoken very well; I do not intend you shall die, at least not for the present, until I know the King's further pleasure." He then continues his narrative:

"After the Judge was gone from the bench, several Protestant gentlemen and others who had heard my trial came to me, though strangers, and told me how sorry they were for me; to whom with thanks I replied, that I was troubled they should grieve for me or my condition, who was joyful for it myself; for I told them I had professed this faith and religion all my lifetime, which I was as sure to be true as I was sure of the truth of *God's* word, on which it was grounded, * * * and I was as ready, by *God's* grace, to die to-morrow, as I had been to receive the sentence of death to-day, and as willingly as if I had a grant of the greatest dukedom."

Before the Judge left *Worcester*, a petition was presented to him from Father *Wall*, acquainting him that he (the prisoner) had had the honour of kissing the King's hand before his Restoration, when in the Low Countries; and his Majesty had promised him and others that when he was restored to the crown they should not live in banishment. The Judge promised to deliver the petition, but it was thought he never did. Father *Wall* was returned to prison, and after some time was sent for up to *London*, as were also several other priests who were under condemnation.

They were all strictly examined; Father *Wall* was declared by his examiner (Mr. *Bedloe*) to be innocent and free from all plots whatever, and he was told that if he would but comply in matters of religion, for all he was condemned, he should not die. To which the father replied, that he would not buy life at so dear a rate as to wrong his conscience. At length, after four months had passed from his condemnation, he was ordered to be executed; and Father *W. Levison,* who visited him in prison, has given the following account of him in a letter preserved by the *English* Franciscans:

"Of late (says he) I was desired, and willingly went, to visit our friend Mr. *Webb* (Father *Wall*), prisoner at *Worcester,* whose execution drew near at hand. I came to him two days before it, and found him a cheerful sufferer of his present imprisonment, and ravished as it were with joy, with the future hopes of dying for so good a cause. I found, contrary to both his and my expectation, the favour of being with him alone; and the day before his execution I enjoyed that privilege for the space of four or five hours together, during which time I heard his confession, and communicated him to his great joy and satisfaction. I ventured likewise, through his desire, to be present at his execution, and placed myself boldly next the under-sheriff, near the gallows, where I had the opportunity of giving him the last absolution, just as he was turned off the ladder. During his imprisonment he carried himself like a true servant and disciple of his crucified Master, thirsting after nothing more than the shedding of his blood for the love of his *God*, which he performed with a courage and cheerfulness becoming a valiant soldier of *Christ*, to the great edification of all Catholics and admiration of all Protestants, the rational and moderate part especially, who showed a great sense of sorrow for his death, decrying the cruelty of putting men to death for priesthood and religion. *He is the first that ever suffered at Worcester since the Catholic religion entered this nation,** which he seemed with joy to tell me before his execution. He was quartered, and his head separated from his body, according to his sentence. His body was permitted to be buried, and was accompanied by the Catholics of the town to St. *Oswald's* churchyard, where he lies interred. His head I got privately and conveyed it to Mr. *Randolph*, who will be careful to keep it till opportunity serves to transport it to *Douay*, &c. The miseries we here lie under are great, and I hope our brothers in safety will be mindful of our condition in their best thoughts, and beg of *God* we may cheerfully bear our crosses, and if it be His holy will, courageously sacrifice our lives in defence of our religion, which is the earnest desire of, &c., *William Levison.* August 25, 1679."

It was on the 22nd of August that Father *Wall* was executed, and the scene of the butchery was probably at *Red Hill*, about a mile out on the

---

* How this mistake could have arisen, when *Oldcorn* was executed at *Worcester* only seventy-three years before, I cannot imagine.

London Road. His head was kept in the cloister of the *English* Friars at *Douay*; and the Catholic writers declared that for some time afterwards, his grave, at St. *Oswald's* burying-ground, appeared green, while the rest of the churchyard was all bare, it being then a constant thoroughfare. Before his death, Father *Wall* composed a long speech, which he delivered to a friend to be printed, in which he declares his faith, hope, and charity, together with his abhorrence of all plots and conspiracies. He implores *God's* mercy for himself, for the church, for king and kingdom, and for his persecutors, whom he forgives, and asks pardon of all whom he might have offended; and finally offers up his death to *God* and commends his soul into His hands.

It seems that the poor priest was interrupted in delivering his speech, " and that which he did speak, being taken by an unskilful scribe, was printed by halves, and so imperfectly, that it was in some places nonsense. To correct that abuse (says his friend), this which he did speak is published by a friend."

I have inspected St. *Oswald's* register, with the view of discovering a memorial of Father *Wall*, but the records do not go so far back, the older ones having been destroyed. *Red Hill* seems to have been the place for the execution of religious and other offenders up to the beginning of the nineteenth century. I believe the laſt execution there was on the 28th July, 1809, when *Patrick Jordan* and *Thomas Brady* were hung for robbing and beating Mr. *C. Bayley*, on *Bromſgrove Lickey*. There is, however, no record of this faɑ̃t in the books of the County Gaol, for it appears that when Mr. *Davies* (predeceſſor of the late Mr. *Lavender*) reſigned the governorſhip of the priſon, he took away all the books and documents with him, and ſold them as private property to *Butler*, the then landlord of the Saracen's Head Inn, by whom they were converted into ſpills for lighting pipes!

The Judge *Atkins* mentioned in the above trial was a native of *Glouceſterſhire*, a Judge of the Court of Common Pleas during the reign of *Charles II*, and Lord Chief Baron after the Revolution; he was an eminent and learned lawyer, much diſtinguiſhed for his attachment to popular rights, and for the uprightneſs and independence of his conduɑ̃t during a period of judicial profligacy and ſubſerviency; nevertheleſs, from his language and conduɑ̃t on the trials of the Jeſuit prieſts and other perſons charged with the Popiſh plot in 1679, he appears to have partaken of the deluſion which pervaded the country reſpeɑ̃ting that tranſaɑ̃tion, and to have played his part in the diſgraceful tragedies then enaɑ̃ted in Weſtminſter Hall.

As an inſtance of the extreme jealouſy and

Catholics. 61

watchfulnefs exercifed over Papifts at this time, it may be ftated that Dame *Mary Yate*, a daughter of the houfe of *Pakington*, who is commemorated on a monument at *Chaddefley* church, and who was then about feventy years old, being a Catholic, on applying for leave to pafs beyond the feas for the benefit of her health, obtained permiffion only after being fenced round by a number of provifos and precautions, to the effect that the faid old lady fhould "give fecurity not to enter into any plott or confpiracy, and fhould not repaire to the cittie of Rome, or returne unto this kingdom, without firft acquainting one of His Majefty's principal Secretaries of State;" and on this condition only was the faid dame "to imbarque with her trunkes of apparel and other neceffaries not prohibited at any porte of this kingdom, and from thence to pafs beyond the feas, provided that fhe depart this kingdom within fourteen dayes." Lady *Mary* was a ftaunch Catholic, and conveyed a large portion of her eftate, to the extent of fome 600*l*. a year, to Father *Conftable*, in truft for the benefit of the clergy at St. *Omer's*, and to pray for her own and her hufband's fouls, &c.

In the parifh books of St. *Nicholas, Worcefter*, there is an entry, in 1679, "For a warrant to take the names of the Papifts, 6*d*." This was probably in confequence of the excitement following the discovery of *Titus Oates's* plot. A subsequent allusion to the Catholics occurs in the same books many years afterwards, when it was "agreed that Papist *Franks's* child be put on the roll," as though it had been a matter of grave deliberation first. Probably this means that belonging to Popish parents precluded children from the benefit of being put on the rolls for parochial relief, but that after some discussion this single case (a pressing one of destitution, no doubt) was admitted. Again, in 1682 —"For paceboard for the excommunicated p'sons, 4d.;" and in 1683 —"charge of the excommunication, 6l. 10s." The above charges were probably for a list of Catholics and others who had been excommunicated in the Ecclesiastical Court here, and which list was fixed to the church door.

James II's accession to the throne gave the Catholics a brief respite, of which the Pope took advantage by dividing *England* into four dioceses, with a Vicar Apostolic to each.

With the year 1685 commences the register of baptism of *Worcester* Catholics, which register is said to be one of the oldest existing among Catholics in *England*. One of the earliest entries in this little book is the following:

"*John Gabriel* was reconciled to ye Church the 6th of March, and having received all ye rites of ye Church, died ye next morning, but remained a week before he was buried, becaufe Parfon *Pye* had excommunicated him for being a Catholic, but at laft he was buried at *Monmouth*."

Among the places named in this regifter as vifited by the priefts of this neighbourhood for the purpofe of adminiftering baptifm, and doubtlefs, too, of offering up the mafs, are the following: *Hindlip*, *Heighmeadow*, Mrs. *Gibbon's* houfe, Mr. *Thomas Gunter's*, *Chepftow Grange*, *Wollafton Grange*, *Collier's*, *Dadmond's*, *Defborough's*, *Day's*, *Goodman's*, *Maunders*, *Writtle Park*, *Weft Grimftead*, *Bofcobel*, &c.

This fame year (the acceffion of *James II*) is believed to have been the date either of the erection or adoption of an exifting houfe on a fite which is now the corner of Pierpoint Street, on the eaft fide of Foregate Street, as a chapel, or oratory, for the Catholics. *Nafh* fays that the chapel was built in that year, and I find in *Oliver's Biography of the Jefuits* that *Henry Humberton (alias Hall)*, who was declared Provincial in 1697, and died 1708, preached a fermon at *Worcefter* in April, 1686, on the fecond Sunday after Eafter, no doubt in the newly-erected chapel. When the King vifited *Worcefter*, in 1687, after attending at the Cathedral on the feaft of St. *Bartholomew*, to gratify fuch as offered themfelves to be touched for the king's evil, His

Majesty went to hear mass at the Popish chapel, on which occasion the Mayor (supposed to be *Shewring*) won immortal praise from the historians of *Worcester* for refusing to accompany the King any further than the doors of the chapel; whereas the corporation records prove that his Worship and the grave and reverend Aldermen, his companions, preferred Protestant guzzling to Catholic religious services, a charge of 2*s.* (equal to nearly 1*l.* of our present money) having been subsequently made on the city funds for their drinking at the Green Dragon, an adjoining inn, during the time of mass. When the King left the chapel, he returned to the Palace, where the good Bishop *Thomas* had provided a princely dinner; but the poor prelate had the mortification to hear a Romish priest ordered to invoke a blessing, and his own offer to perform that part of his duty rejected by the King, who said he would spare him that trouble, for that he had a chaplain of his own. No doubt the poor Bishop turned away with a tear in his eye and a sinking in his heart at the foresight of coming troubles.

Bishop *Thomas*, however, remained true to his unworthy master; for though he refused to read and circulate the King's memorable declaration as to the suspension of the penal laws against nonconformists, in June, 1688, and for which he incurred the severe displeasure of the Court, he subsequently declined to take the oath of allegiance to *William III*, and actually vacated his fee rather than abandon that duty which he believed was owing to the unfortunate *James*. But the fate of this wretched monarch was soon decided; and at the Revolution of 1688, although King *William* allowed the unrepealed acts against Catholics to sink partially into abeyance, he subsequently passed an act to prevent the growth of Popery, by which a reward of 100*l*. was offered for apprehending any priest or Jesuit.

To show the sense of the people of *Worcester*, at the time of the landing of the Prince of *Orange*, it may be stated that the *Worcester* Corporation then passed a resolution as follows:

"We, the Mayor, Aldermen, Sheriff, Town Council, and citizens of the city of *Worcester*, whose names are subscribed, do declare that to our utmost endeavours in our several stations and places we will aid and assist His Highness the Prince of *Orange*, and all those that shall oppose the desperate attempts and conspiracies of the Papists and their adherents, and to the hazard of our lives will preserve His Majesty's most sacred person, uphold the Protestant religion by law established, and maintain the ancient liberties of this kingdom."

Catholic chapels were now everywhere ruthlessly destroyed; that at *Worcester* no doubt sharing the same fate. *Macaulay* states that when the *Dutch* army was marching from *Torbay* towards *London,* in 1688, Sir *E. Harley,* of *Brampton Brian,* and his son *Robert* (afterwards, as Earl of *Oxford,* Queen *Anne's* minister, and a high churchman), declared for the Prince of *Orange* and a free Parliament, raised a large body of horse, took possession of *Worcester,* and evinced their zeal against Popery by publicly breaking to pieces, in the High Street, a piece of sculpture which to rigid precisians seemed idolatrous.

But however relentlessly the Catholics were pursued at this period, no blood was shed; another step had been gained in the progress of religious liberty, and the ancient disputes now took a controversial turn. Dr. *Stillingfleet,* Bishop of *Worcester,* who is said to have had " no equal in ecclesiastical learning, was an elegant preacher and a masterly disputant, exercised himself in several noted controversies, and with a reputation of advantage. He was a victorious combatant of Papists, dissenters, and Socinians, and no unequal opponent of the great *Locke.* He may be accounted the *Bellarmine* of the Church of *England.*"

There were at that time in *Worcester* province 719 Papists above the age of sixteen, the proportion of conformists to nonconformists being nearly twenty-three to one, and of conformists to Papists 179 to one. In the reign of *James II* there were Franciscans in *Worcester* (as Father *Waterworth* informs me), but when they came, where they resided, or how long they remained, are questions to which I can find no answer.

About the period 1701-4, Father *Russell*, a Jesuit, was serving in " St. *George's* residence, *Worcester;* " and in 1708, Father *Beeston*. The latter was educated at St. *Omer's*, made his solemn vows of religion in 1698, and was sent to the *Worcester* mission, but recalled in 1708 to *Watton*, to fill the post of master of the novices, and died at St. *Omer's* in 1732.

In the *Georgian* era the persecution of the Catholics was continued. *Walpole* visited " reputed Papists" with heavy taxes on their lands and estates, and all Catholics were compelled, within six months of their coming of age, to register their names and estates with the Clerk of the Peace, otherwise their possessions were forfeited; and as late as the year 1769 the Hon. *James Talbot* was tried for his life at the Old Bailey for saying mass, and only escaped through want of evidence. In those days, if a Catholic travelled by waggon or stage coach he was wise if he held his tongue on religious matters, so intense was still the national feeling against Popery: the proscribed party were at the mercy of any one who wished to injure or insult them, and every neighbouring magistrate was too willing at a moment's notice to tender the oath so obnoxious to their feelings. The Test and Corporation Acts, too, had long excluded them from all offices. There are some probably still living who remember the difficulties and privations with which the Catholics had to contend at the close of the last century---how they were driven to have their chapels secluded and to go to them in a circuitous way to avoid suspicion: if their meeting house was in the country (as at *Blackmoor Park*, near *Malvern*) it was a mere upper room, and a trusty watchman was stationed near at hand to prevent the approach of suspicious parties; while in towns they often assembled in stables or public houses under the guise of a club, and with pots of beer before them to mislead the domestics, but when left to themselves they would pursue their devotions. On the whole, however, Catholics breathed more freely than before, and were enabled to establish schools, one of which (by the Benedictines) was at *Redmarley*, in this county, and another at *Sedgley Park*, near *Wolverhampton*, in a mansion belonging to the Lord *Dudley and Ward*. In 1768, this establishment was transferred to Dr. *Hornyold*, Vicar Apostolic of the Midland District; he was a descendant of the *Hornyolds* of *Hanley Castle*, and having studied and received ordination at *Douay*, he entered upon his first mission at *Grantham*, and soon became remarkable for zeal and courage. Once, in the midſt of a terrible ſtorm, he was informed that one of his flock who lived at a diſtance was in danger of death, whereupon he immediately ſet out, and ſwam his horſe through a river ſwollen with the flood, to the imminent danger both of horſe and rider. On another occaſion, a conſtable coming to ſeize him as a Catholic prieſt, juſt when he was concluding maſs, barely ſufficient time was allowed him to ſave himſelf by ſubſtituting a female cap for his flowing periwig, and throwing a woman's cloak over his veſtments; in this diſguiſe he placed himſelf in the corner of a room, and was paſſed by unnoticed. His diſtrict extended from *Yarmouth* to the *Malvern Hills* and *Weſt Shropſhire*, and from *Barton-on-Humber* and *North Derbyſhire* to *Oxford* and *Henley*. Dr. *Hornyold* was aſſiduous in viſiting every part of his charge; he was an abſtemious and a cheerful man; *obiit* December, 1778.

The Jeſuits who ſucceeded Father *Beeſton* at *Worceſter* were *William Baxter* (real name *Caſe*), *Felix Bartlett*, and *Richard Clough*. The firſt was a native of *Lancaſhire*, and joined the Society of *Jeſus* in 1711. After many years' employment in this miſſion, *Oliver* ſays, "he was called to receive his retribution at *Worceſter*, July 13th, 1747, aged fifty-ſeven." This probably means nothing more than a natural death, for I find no trace of his having come to a violent end. *Bartlett* was born March 19th, 1708, probably at *Worcester*, where his mother proved herself a generous friend of the Jesuits. At the age of eighteen he enrolled himself among the children of St. *Ignatius*, and in 1740 was elevated to the rank of a professed father. *Worcester* was his chief residence, and here he ended his mortal career in 1777. *Richard Clough* was born November 28th, 1728, and at the age of sixteen dedicated himself to *God* in the Society of Jesuits; nineteen years afterwards he was promoted to the rank of a professed father, and for a considerable time (says *Oliver*) he was "incumbent of *Worcester*, where he built the late chapel." Dying here on the 19th of January, 1777, his remains were deposited in St. *Oswald's* cemetery. *William Walmesley*, another Jesuit father, who was born in *Lancashire* in 1712, is said to have died at *Worcester* in 1769.

In the baptismal register before alluded to, distinct reference is made to the Catholic chapel at *Worcester* on the 12th of March, 1749. Perhaps the chapel was still in Foregate Street, for mention is made of a baptism in Foregate Street, at Mr. *Berkeley's*, in 1776, and probably the chapel was attached to Mr. *Berkeley's* house; yet all the local historians and guide books say that the Catholics had a chapel on the site of the present building in "Sansome Row," or, as it was sometimes described, "Sansome Fields," ever since the year 1764. That chapel was, no doubt, the one erected by Father *Clough* (as mentioned above), the former chapel at Mr. *Berkeley's* house still remaining as a private oratory.

Thomas Sanders succeeded *Richard Clough*, and died at *Worcester*, November, 1790; he was assisted by one *Wharton* (cousin to Archbishop *Carroll*), who seceded to the Protestant Church and went to *America*. During the incumbency of *Sanders*, too, Father *Bernard Cross* died at *Worcester*, in 1785; he was born at *Teneriffe* in 1715, and on his twenty-second birthday consecrated himself to *God* in the Society of Jesuits; he was admitted to the " profession of the four vows " on the Feast of the Assumption, 1755; for some time he exercised his missionary functions at *Vera Cruz*, and was for several years stationed in *London* before his coming to *Worcester*.

All this while the spirit of persecution slept not, until the prospect of the dangers of the *American* war rendered it necessary to consult the goodwill and patriotism of all sects : then the Catholics were indulged (in 1778) by a repeal of most of their severest disabilities. Protestant apprehension, however, became greatly aroused by this leniency, and *Wesley* is accused of having "hounded on" the popular cry against the Catholics; the Lord *George Gordon* riots ensued, and after that event a large portion of the Catholic party wavered in their submission to *Rome*, sought favour of the Protestants and those in power, and many went over to the well-endowed establishment. *Billinge*, the chaplain at *Moseley*, and *Wharton* (before-mentioned), who was serving the mission at *Worcester*, were said to have been among these worldly-minded: both were successful musicians, became fond of company, who applauded their performances, and both fell. *Billinge*, on the last Sunday on which he said mass, told his people at *Moseley* that if they saw anything strange in him they should remember what he had taught them but not follow his example. They understood the meaning of this when they heard, on the next Sunday, that he had publicly apostatised; he afterwards married, and held the living of *Wombourn*. This is the account which Catholic writers give of these two men.

With regard to *Wharton*, I find that he became a Protestant about the year 1779, and resided, until 1784, in the house attached to the Catholic chapel in Sansome Fields. He left this country for *America*, where, on his arrival, he published *A Letter to the Roman Catholics of Worcester, from the late Chaplain to that Society,*

C. H. Wharton, ſtating the motives which had induced him to relinquiſh their communion and become a member of the Proteſtant Church, denying the infallibility of Pope or Church, aſſerting the right of private judgment, oppoſing celibacy, &c. This pamphlet (which I have ſeen in the *Britiſh* Muſeum) was anſwered by Mr. *Wharton's* couſin, Archbiſhop *Carroll*, and gave riſe to conſiderable controverſy, carried on in print. The Rev. *Arthur Vaughan*, ſucceſſor to Rev. *Charles Dodd*, as Catholic prieſt at *Harvington*, in this county, publiſhed *The Ghoſt of Sanſome Fields*, *on occaſion of Mr. Wharton's abandoning his Flock at Worceſter;* and Mr. *John Hawkins*, who alſo conformed to the Proteſtant Church in 1779 from having been a monk, and ſoon afterwards married the eldeſt daughter of *R. Burney*, Eſq., of *Barbourne* Lodge, alſo publiſhed two works: 1. *A Letter from a Catholic Chriſtian to his Roman Catholic Friend, ſtating the Reaſon for his Relinquiſhing the Communion of the Church of Rome; Worceſter*, 1780; and 2. *An Eſſay on the Law of Celibacy impoſed on the Clergy of the Roman Catholic Church, interſperſed with various remarks upon ſeveral other parts of their diſcipline; alſo a few remarks on Mr. Carroll's Anſwer to the Roman Catholics of the United States of America, occaſioned by Mr. Wharton's Letter, in which he had ſtated his*

Reasons for Relinquishing the Communion of the Church of Rome; 1784-5, 4s.6d.:" and other works.

In the year 1791 a bill was passed repealing various statutes and tolerating the schools and the religious worship of Catholics; and in the same year I find that *Robert Berkeley* of *Spetchley, T. Hornyold* the younger of *Blackmoor Park, John Baynham* of *Purshall* Hall, clerk, *Thomas Parker* of *Heath Green, Beoley,* and *Mary Williams* of *Little Malvern,* subscribed certificates that they had set apart rooms in their respective houses for *Roman* Catholic worship. In 1796, *Andrew Robinson,* clerk, of *Grafton Manor,* and *Richard Cornthwaite,* clerk, of *Harvington* Hall, *Chaddesley,* set apart rooms for the same purpose.

Eight thousand exiled priests were driven into *England* by the great *French* Revolution; and though most of them returned in the following year, in consequence of *Pius VII* treating with *Napoleon,* those who remained here denounced the Pope's arrangement as schismatical, and a serious division took place in the Catholic party. *Pius* became *Napoleon's* captive, and did not regain his liberty till the year 1814, when it was actually to the Protestant bayonets of the *British* troops that His Holiness owed his protection at *Genoa,* when the Emperor escaped from *Elba.* All this while the *British* Parliament had been entertaining bills for the emancipation of the Catholics and for establishing a Protestant veto on their appointment of bishops. Then it was that *Sydney Smith* launched his famous invectives against the penal statutes, as being the most cruel and atrocious system of persecution ever instituted by one religious body against another; and this paved the way for the relief of 1829.

During the *French* Revolution, and up to the period of the emancipation, the names of Jesuits and priests stationed at *Worcester* were---*Williams, Morris, Robinson, Norris, Tristram, Leadbetter,* and *Sewell. Joseph Williams* (whose family name was *Gittings*) was born in 1744, admitted a Jesuit in 1762, died at *Worcester* on Lady Day, 1797, and was buried at St. *Oswald's. John Morris* was born in *Lancashire* in 1770. Soon after his receiving holy orders his services were bestowed on the *Worcester* mission, where he arrived for the Easter of 1797.

" Here (says *Oliver)* this zealous and most disinterested man deserved to be regarded as the father of the poor. Naturally bashful and retired, yet in the circle of his immediate acquaintance his conversation abounded with information, and was enlivened and enriched with sprightly humour and anecdote. It pleased Almighty *God* to purify his servant by a long and painful illness, which he endured with edifying patience, resignation, and fortitude. He was released from his sufferings about four p.m. on Sunday, 3rd of October, 1830, and was buried in the cemetery of the new chapel."

Andrew Robinson was born in *Yorkshire* in 1741, admitted to the Society of *Jesuits* in 1763, and after serving the *English* mission for nearly sixty years, he closed his lengthened career at *Worcester*, in February, 1826. *N. Sewell* was born in 1745 in *Maryland*, became a *Jesuit* in 1766, and in 1821 was Provincial, but resigning his office five or six years afterwards, he proceeded to *Worcester*, to assist his valued friend, Rev. *Joseph Tristram*, and had the comfort of seeing a new, large, and handsome chapel opened in this city on the 16th of July, 1829. He died on the 14th of March, 1834, at the patriarchal age of eighty-nine, and was buried in the cemetery adjoining the chapel.

The year 1829 must have afforded a great triumph to the Catholics, especially of *Worcester*, in witnessing the success of the Emancipation Bill and the erection of their new chapel. The " Right Rev. Dr. *Walsh*, Vicar Apostolic of the Midland District," officiated at the opening ceremonies, assisted by the Very Rev. Dr. *Weedall*, President of *Oscot* College, the Rev. Mr. *Morgan*, Sub-Deacon, and numerous of the Catholic clergy. Grand high mass was celebrated, and Dr. *Weedall* preached in defence of the ordinance of the mass and the doctrine of the real presence, his text being—" *Christ* our paſſover is ſacrificed for us." In the afternoon the Rev. Prelate addreſſed the congregation from the altar, explaining ſome of the fundamental doctrines of the Church of *Rome*, and diſavowing many of the obnoxious tenets attributed to its profeſſors by thoſe who diſſented from her precepts, eſpecially thoſe relating to the keeping faith with heretics. The ſum of 48*l.* was collected.

Before the Catholic relief meaſure was paſſed, a great ſtruggle took place throughout the country, in which *Worceſterſhire* fully participated. An addreſs to the King and petitions againſt Catholic emancipation, agreed upon at a meeting at the *Worceſter* Guildhall, were each ſigned by upwards of 6000 perſons; and in the *Dudley* petition the column of ſignatures meaſured 230 feet. Of theſe ſignatures three were actually thoſe of Catholics, the writers obſerving—" We have liberty enough already, and thoſe who want more want it for no good." By the Emancipation Bill, Catholics were ſtill forbidden to aſſume the title of Proteſtant ſees; all *Jeſuits* and monaſtic orders were to be ſuppreſſed, and numerous penalties were allowed to remain on the ſtatute book; yet nearly all theſe have become obſolete. The *Oxford* tractarian movement is the next feature to be noticed in connection with the progreſs of Catholiciſm: *Ward*, *Puſey*, and *Newman*, did their work, and the *Romish* Church reaped a rich harvest. In the year 1840 the Vicars Apostolic in *England* were increased from four to eight, as a preparation for a further change, namely, the restoration of the hierarchy; and after much heat and dissension among the people, this step was achieved in 1850, when the whole kingdom, together with *Wales*, was formed into a province, containing one metropolitan see of *Westminster* and twelve suffragan sees.

The names of the Jesuits and priests who have been located at *Worcester* since the opening of the new chapel in 1829 are---*Postlewhite*, *Rigby*, *Brownbill*, *McClune*, *C. Lomax*, *Chadwick*, *W. Lomax*, *Jarrett*, *Beeston*, *Bateman*, *Corr*, *Swale*, *Holden*, *Bird*, *Laurenson*, *Cooper*, *F. Jarrett*, *W. Waterworth*, and *Meagher*, the two latter being the priests now (1860) in residence here.

Among the Jesuits and other Catholics (not mentioned in the foregoing account) connected with the city and county of *Worcester* were---*Francis Young* of *Worcestershire*, who, quitting *Oxford*, entered the *English* College at *Rome* in 1598. He is described as "a good controversial father." *Richard Bristow* was born at *Worcester* and educated at *Oxford*, where he and *Campion* entertained Queen *Elizabeth* with a public disputation, and acquitted themselves so as to gain much applause. He shortly afterwards conformed to the

Church of *Rome*, and was invited by the famous *Allen*, afterwards Cardinal, to *Douay*, where he diftinguifhed himfelf in the *Englifh* College, as he alfo did fubfequently at *Rheims*. *Briftow* is faid to have "rivalled *Allen* in prudence, *Stapleton* in acutenefs, *Campion* in eloquence, *Wright* in theology, and *Martin* in languages." His death was occafioned by fevere application to his ftudies. *William Morton*, born in *Worcefterfhire* in 1597, admitted among the Jefuits at the age of thirty-three, and is thus defcribed—"*Juvat noftros in Anglia multiplici minifterio;*" *obiit* 1667. *John Harrifon*, born in *Worcefterfhire* in 1615, and died at the age of fixty-three. *John Mace*, a "temporal coadjutor," was alfo a native of *Worcefterfhire*; he died at *Rome* 14th September, 1689, aged fixty-nine. *James Lane*, born in *Worcefterfhire* in 1737, admitted a *Jefuit* at the age of twenty-one, and paffed through his ftudies with diftinguifhed honours; he refided at *Norwich* for half a century, and died in 1821. Laftly, *Clement Weetman*, born in *Staffordfhire* in 1781, and taking upon himfelf the *Grafton* miffion, died at *Worcefter* in 1813, and was buried at St. *Ofwald's*.

The number of Jefuits in this province at prefent (1860) is fuppofed to be about 260; of thefe, however, only one-half are yet priefts. The *Worcefter* congregation of Catholics number nearly 1500, but many of thefe live out of the city, and many are *Irifh*.

It will thus be seen how this proscribed church passed through the fiery ordeal which they had for so lengthened a period administered to others, and how they gradually emerged from their oppressed condition to breathe with something of the freedom enjoyed by their fellow creatures. The rancour of the national hatred seems at length to have died out, and left the work of conversion to be effected by argument and holy example rather than by the faggot or the gallows. Even so let it be; for, as the author of *The Ingle Nook* observes, " The humble, the meek, the merciful, the just, the pious, and the devout, are everywhere of one religion; and when Death has taken off the mask they will know one another, though the liveries they wear here make them strangers."

www.ingramcontent.com/pod-product-compliance
Lightning Source LLC
Chambersburg PA
CBHW031410160426
43196CB00007B/966